Anne of
Cleves

About the Author

Elizabeth Norton gained her first degree from the University of Cambridge, and her Masters from the University of Oxford. Her other books include *Anne Boleyn, Jane Seymour: Henry VIII's True Love, Catherine Parr* (all published by Amberley Publishing) and *She Wolves: The Notorious Queens of England*. She lives in Kingston Upon Thames.

Also by Elizabeth Norton:

Forthcoming titles from Elizabeth Norton:

Anne of Cleves

Henry VIII's Discarded Bride

ELIZABETH NORTON

AMBERLEY

To my sister, Jo
With thanks to Stefanie and Renate Worden

This edition first published 2010

Amberley Publishing Plc
Cirencester Road, Chalford,
Stroud, Gloucestershire, GL6 8PE

www.amberleybooks.com

Copyright © Elizabeth Norton, 2009, 2010

The right of Elizabeth Norton to be identified as the Author
of this work has been asserted in accordance with the
Copyrights, Designs and Patents Act 1988.

British Library Cataloguing in Publication Data.
A catalogue record for this book is available from the British Library.

ISBN 978 1 4456 0183 0

Typesetting and Origination by Amberley Publishing.
Printed in Great Britain.

Contents

The Relationship Between the House of Cleves and the House of Burgundy

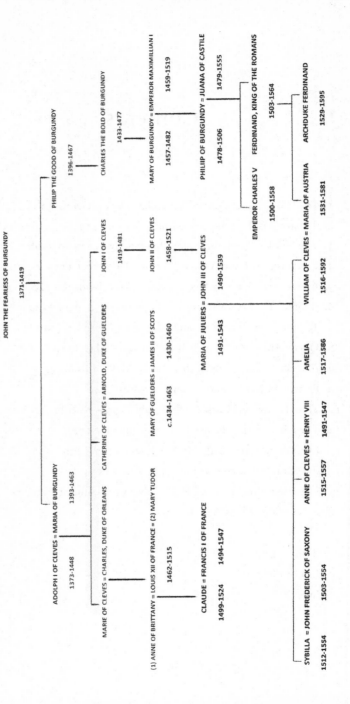

I

The Daughter of Cleves:
September 1515 – October 1537

The woman who would become Henry VIII's fourth wife, was born into a princely German family during the early years of her future husband's reign. No one, seeing Anne of Cleves during her childhood, could ever have imagined that she would, for a few brief months, become a queen, or end her life as the last surviving spouse of England's most married monarch, and one of the most notorious men in Europe. Anne of Cleves survived her disastrous marriage to remain on good terms with the king and in high favour and, while Henry left a widow, it was Anne who truly was the wife who survived.

Anne of Cleves was born at Dusseldorf on 22 September 1515, the second daughter of John III, Duke of Cleves and his wife, Maria of Juliers. The baby's sex was something of a disappointment for her parents, leaving their three-year-old daughter Sibylla as heiress to their lands. Less than a year later Anne's birth was followed by that of a brother, William. In 1517 the family was completed by the birth of a third sister, Amelia. All four children spent their early years under their mother's care before William, as the heir, was removed from the company of his sisters to be educated as a future duke of Juliers-Cleves.

With the exception of Catherine of Aragon, Anne of Cleves had the grandest lineage of any of Henry VIII's wives. She was descended from both the kings of England, through a daughter of Edward I, and the kings of France. On her father's side she was also closely related to Louis XII of France, who had died just over nine months before her birth, and to the Dukes of Burgundy. Anne's father, Duke John III, ruled the small duchies of Cleves and Mark in the lower Rhine valley in an area in Germany close to the modern Dutch border. The area ruled by her father was only around 2,000 square miles in size but was populous and wealthy. Although Cleves-Mark was a part of the Holy Roman Empire, it was essentially independent and John III was an important German ruler.

John III's ancestors, the Counts of Mark, had come into possession of the wealthier Cleves through marriage in the mid-fourteenth century. The combined power of the two areas led to the counts being created dukes in the early fifteenth century, bringing them to international importance in central Europe. This prominence was further increased when Anne's great-great-grandfather, Adolph I, Duke of Cleves, married Maria, sister of the powerful Duke Philip the Good of Burgundy.

By the mid-fifteenth century, Burgundy was the most opulent and wealthy country in Europe and Philip the Good took a personal interest in his sister's children. It was this connection which allowed Mary of Guelders, granddaughter of Adolph I and Maria of Burgundy, to marry James II of Scotland. An even grander match was arranged for Adolph I's daughter, Marie, who married the Duke of Orleans. Their son, the future Louis XII of France, was raised in Orleans by his mother. Louis XII would later marry Mary Tudor, younger sister of Henry VIII, and, through his daughter, Claude, was the ancestor of most of the sixteenth-century kings of France, making them distantly Anne's cousins. Marie of Cleves, like many of the Cleves women, was no beauty, being described by a Bohemian visitor to her court as 'a woman of but very moderate looks'. She was, however strong-willed and intelligent, qualities that Anne also possessed.

Philip the Good of Burgundy was particularly attached to his nephew, John I of Cleves. John spent much of his time in Burgundy and was made a knight of the famous order of the Golden Fleece by his uncle. Membership of the order was limited to twenty-five and it was the ambition of many princes in Europe. John I experienced firsthand the splendours of the Burgundian court which so amazed foreign visitors. In 1468, when the sister of the English king, Edward IV, was sent to Burgundy to marry Philip's son, Charles the Bold, one member of her entourage wrote expansively on the pageants and jousts held in her honour, with the participants richly dressed in 'clothe of gold and sylk and sylvyr, and goldsmyths werk'. He was amazed at the great plenty there, musing that 'as for the Dwkys coort, as of lords, ladys and gentylwomen, knyts, sqwyers, and gentlymen I hert never of non lyek to it, save kyng Artourys court'. It is perhaps no wonder that John I's father, Adolph I mocked his son when he returned to the less ostentatious court of Cleves, commenting on his son's courtly way of speaking: 'Here comes Johnny with the bark (or noise).'

While, by the time of Anne's birth, the Burgundian connection with Cleves was remote, it provided Anne with blood ties to most of the greatest princes in Europe. Cleves was also linked to the Burgundian ducal family as late as 1507 when, during a rebellion in the Netherlands following the death of Mary of Burgundy the heiress of Charles the Bold, Mary's widower, the Emperor Maximillian, was only released from captivity when a relative of Anne's, Philip of Cleves, agreed to stand as hostage in his stead. The relationship became somewhat strained when, during his imprisonment, Philip abandoned Maximillian for the French. Nonetheless, when Maximillian and Mary of Burgundy's grandson, Charles V succeeded to the Netherlands and as Emperor in 1519 the remote connection to Burgundy meant that Anne of Cleves was a distant kinswoman of the most powerful man in Europe. Anne's father, John III, also maintained relations with his powerful cousin and he was one of the noblemen who accompanied Charles on his visit to England in May 1522, crossing to Dover from Calais and then following the same route to London that his daughter would take just under eighteen years later.

Anne may have had some memory of her grandfather, John II, Duke of Cleves, who died in 1521. John II inherited something of his father's opulent tastes and was nicknamed 'the Babymaker' for his sixty-three illegitimate children, all fathered before he married Anne's grandmother, Mechtild of Hesse at the age of thirty-one. With John II's enormous family, Anne must also have been used to finding her father's court and the cities that she visited populated with her uncles, aunts and cousins. Anne's own father, John III, who succeeded as Duke of Cleves in 1521, was a much less flamboyant character, nicknamed instead 'the Simple'. A visitor to John III's court in 1537 commented that Anne's father had a taste for extravagant clothes but had little intelligence and this probably accounts for the nickname.

Whatever his intelligence, or lack of it, John III made a brilliant marriage. In 1496 the Emperor Maximillian had recognized Maria, the only child of the Duke of Juliers-Berg as the heiress to both duchies. Juliers and Berg, with a combined size of nearly 4,000 square miles, dwarfed the smaller Cleves-Mark and neighboured John III's lands. Through John III and Maria's marriage the four territories were combined to create a strategically important powerbase on both sides of the Rhine. Although she was a strong-minded woman, Anne's mother, Maria, never asserted her rights to Julier-Berg and was ostensibly content for her husband and son to rule her lands for her. However, she had a great deal of influence over her son. The Emperor Charles V himself believed that William 'followed the council of his mother' and in 1540 while negotiating with Charles, William himself noted that he could not take any final decision until he had consulted with his mother.

Maria was responsible for the upbringing and education of her daughters. In the early sixteenth century it had become fashionable to educate girls, but this idea had not reached Duchess Maria in Cleves. Maria was determined to equip her daughters for their future roles as wives for German princes and Anne received a notably restricted education from an English viewpoint. According to the English ambassador, Nicholas Wotton, in 1539, Anne:

> Hathe from her childehode (lyke as the ladye Sybille was, tyll she wer maryed, and the ladye Amelye hathe ben and is) ben brought up withe the ladye Duchesse her mother, and yn maner never from her ellebow, the ladye Duchesse being a wysse ladye, and one that verye streytelye lookithe to her children. All the gentylmenne of the courte, and other that I have askyd of, rapport her [Anne] to be of verye lowlye and gentyll condicions, by the whiche she hathe so muche wonne her mothers favour, that she is verye lothe to suffer her to departe from her.

Anne was a particular favourite of her strict mother and stayed by her side during her childhood and early adulthood, spending her time at her needlework. She was able to read and write but knew no languages save her native German. This in itself was not an entire disadvantage and, while Henry VIII is known to have been attracted to clever women, his third, and perhaps favourite wife Jane Seymour received an education as limited as Anne's. Unfortunately, given Anne's later marriage to the musical king, she was not taught to sing or play an instrument, 'for they take it here yn Germanye for a rebuke and an occasion of lightenesse that great ladyes shuld be lernyd or have enye knowledge of musike'. In spite of the limitations in Anne's education, the English ambassador noted that 'her witte is so goode, that no doubte she wille in a shorte space lerne th'Englissh tongue, when so ever she puttithe her mynde to hit'. Anne's mother gave her daughters the best upbringing that she could to fit them for life as the wives of dukes and princes, but it was very far from what would have been ideal for Anne as a future queen of England.

There has always been some dispute over Anne's religious views with a number of modern writers inaccurately describing her as a Lutheran. Anne's mother, who was responsible for Anne's religious education, was a devout Catholic. John III was influenced by the religious reform but he looked towards the humanist Erasmus, rather than Luther, remaining in outlook very much a Catholic, although a reformed one. In 1533 John III created a set of church regulations which he took to Erasmus for approval. He also asked Erasmus to recommend a tutor for William who, unlike his sisters, was given a fine education. John III's religious views were very close to Henry VIII's with neither Cleves nor England recognizing the pope's authority. In spite of this neither country was by any means Protestant by the 1530s.

Anne's eldest sister, Sibylla, was famed for her beauty. It was a loss to Anne and her younger sister, Amelia, when Sibylla left their family group to marry at the age of fourteen in 1527. Sibylla's marriage to John Frederick, the eldest son of the powerful Duke of Saxony, was a prestigious one. Saxony was very strongly Lutheran. The Protestant reformation had a major impact on the German states and, by 1530, it had effectively divided the Holy Roman Empire in two. While Anne's father was happy to deal with both Catholics and Protestants, much of Germany was not so enlightened. The breach between Protestant Germany and the emperor finally came in January 1531 when Charles V secured the election of his brother, Ferdinand, as King of the Romans, effectively naming him as his heir as Holy Roman Emperor. Ferdinand was as staunchly Catholic as his brother and the election caused consternation in Germany. In the summer of 1530 Charles had summoned an Imperial Diet at Augsburg to try to resolve the religious differences, for which the Protestants produced the Confession of Augsburg, a comprehensive statement of their faith. This was ignored by the emperor who continued to call for the Protestants to return to the Catholic church, something that alarmed the duchy of Saxony and other German states. In response to this, the representatives of six German princes and ten city states met at the town of Schmalkalden in late 1530 and in February 1531 they concluded a treaty to provide for the formation of a defensive league known as the Schmalkaldic League. The League was to prove a major presence in European politics for over fifteen years and it was led by Philip, Landgrave of Hesse, and Anne's own brother-in-law, John Frederick Duke of Saxony, providing Cleves with strong links to the League, even if religious differences precluded them from joining it. The formation of the League and Anne's close links to its leaders, increased her prominence on the European marriage market.

Sibylla's marriage to John Frederick was an excellent match and John III was generous in the terms of the marriage treaty, providing her with a dowry of 25,000 florins. He also covenanted with John Frederick that, in the event that William died without sons, John Frederick would become heir to Cleves, on the understanding that he would pay 160,000 florins 'towards the marriage of the other daughters, wherof there be now two living'. John III was already thinking of Anne's marriage as he completed the arrangements for Sibylla's and, in 1527 he came to an agreement concerning her future. According to the report of Henry Olisleger, Vice-Chancellor of Cleves:

The old Duke of Cleves and the Duke of Lorayne hadde ben yn communicacion together for the mariaige of the Marquyse, the duke of Loraynes sonne, and the said Ladye Anne, and that they hadde gone so ferre that wrytinges wer made and sealyd up on hit, and that the duke of Cleves

hadde payed thereupon to the duke of Gheldres by the said agreement
certeyn sommes of money, and hadde fulfilled on his part all things, saving
that the lady Anne was not yet maryed to the said Marquyse.

Anne's betrothal to Francis, heir to the Duchy of Lorraine was an entirely
political bargain and she never even met her betrothed. The marriage
was brokered by Charles of Egmond, the Duke of Guelders, a duchy that
neighboured Juliers-Cleves. Guelders had originally belonged to the dukes
of Juliers but had been lost in the fifteenth century. Charles of Egmond
was childless and, by 1527, Guelders was claimed by his nephew the Duke
of Lorraine, by John III as the husband of Maria of Juliers, by Charles
V and even by Francis I of France. In the negotiations of 1527, it was
agreed that, in return for John III passing his claim to Guelders to Anne,
she would marry Francis of Lorraine who would be recognized as heir to
Guelders. The marriage contract was signed on 5 June 1527 when Anne
was eleven but neither she nor Francis were ever called upon to give their
consents to the match, something that would have made the betrothal
binding. By August 1539 the English ambassador was able to report: 'I find
the Counsell willing yn nough to publisshe and manifeste to the world,
that by eny covenauntes made by th'olde Duke of Cleves and the Duke of
Lorayne, my lady Anne is not bownden; but ever hathe ben and yet is at
her free libertye to marye where ever she wille.'

Anne's betrothal to Francis of Lorraine was entirely tied up with the fate
of Guelders. Charles of Egmond had a difficult relationship with Charles
V who maintained that the Duke of Guelders had no right to the province.
According to Charles V himself:

Some time previously Count Charles of Egmont had died, after having for
many years ruled the duchy of Gueldres, which, however, did not belong to
him. More than that, he had seized upon every opportunity to develop and
increase his power, and at various periods he had attempted to get possession
of Friesland, Overyssel, and Groningen, from which he was always driven
back by the Imperialists, and which territories were in the peaceful possession
of His Majesty [Charles V].

Charles of Egmond spent much of his time as Duke of Guelders at war with the emperor and, as a result, constantly changed his views as to who should succeed him. In 1527 he had favoured Francis of Lorraine but, at other times, he named Francis I of France as his successor. In 1538 he bequeathed the duchy to Anne's brother, William, and died in June of that year, before he had a chance to change his mind. After years of war, Guelders was not wealthy, but its acquisition gave Juliers-Cleves vital access to the sea and William rushed to take possession of the duchy, putting himself in opposition to the emperor. The move also had profound consequences for Anne and when, in February 1539, ambassadors from the Duke of Lorraine arrived at Cleves in an attempt to bring into force Anne's marriage treaty and so ensure that Guelders was transferred to Francis of Lorraine, any chance that Anne would ever marry Francis of Lorraine was finally brought to an end as William had no intention of giving up his new acquisition without a fight.

William's acquisition of Guelders turned Charles V's attention towards him for the first time and the emperor himself recorded that:

> after the death of Charles of Egmont, Duke William of Cleves seized upon the government of the duchy of Guelders, asserting a claim to it. His Imperial Majesty, seeing how matters stood, and how he consequently ought to and could act, made him offers, the conditions of which were such that they ought reasonably to have been accepted.

William did not see it that way and looked around for allies to support him. He naturally looked toward his brother-in-law, John Frederick, and also towards England where the king, Henry VIII, was also at odds with the emperor.

Throughout Anne's childhood and early adulthood there had been some attempts at opening contact with Henry VIII in Germany. In 1514 Henry VIII had supplied troops for the emperor's war with Guelders but by the 1530s they were implacably opposed. The Duke of Saxony made the first move by sending ambassadors to Henry in late 1529, though the king had already received reports of German friendship towards him earlier in that year. The Schmalkaldic League also made early attempts to establish a relationship with England and, in February 1531, sent ambassadors to the king. Contact continued throughout the 1530s although no alliance was ever negotiated.

Anne's father was also involved in the negotiations with England and, in 1530, it was suggested to Henry that a marriage alliance with Cleves could be to his advantage. According to one report, by a German, Herman Ringk, an alliance with the Duke of Cleves was particularly recommended as he 'possesses three most powerful duchies and two earldoms, and many towns not only strong but populous. If England were in danger he could alone raise an army sufficient to defend it, and he is descended from the same stock as the kings of England, as will be shown by a genealogy'. Although the proposed alliance was not expressly stated, it was most likely intended to be between William and Henry's daughter, Princess Mary. The report continued that 'the Duke had but one son, though he has three daughters. His son is fifteen years old, of middle height, brown complexion, sound in body and limbs well learned, and speaks Latin and French'. Nothing came of the proposal but a marriage with Cleves remained a possibility in Henry's mind.

In 1537 another marriage alliance was to be suggested between England and Cleves although this one was put forward by the English themselves and directly affected Anne. For, in October 1537, Henry VIII began his search for a fourth wife.

2

A Warren of Honourable Ladies:
October 1537 – January 1539

Jane Seymour, the third wife of Henry VIII, died on 24 October 1537 only twelve days after giving birth to the king's son and heir. Henry was genuinely grief-stricken at her death but there is no doubt that, for him, the survival of his son outweighed the death of the queen. After nearly twenty years on the throne Henry finally had his heir. In spite of this, everyone, including the king, knew that the succession could never be secure with only one infant heir.

Previously, Henry had selected a new wife before disposing of his spouse but Jane's death took him by surprise and he had no English candidate to step into her place. Henry's marriage to two Englishwomen, Anne Boleyn and Jane Seymour caused surprise both in England and on the continent. Henry's grandfather, Edward IV, had married an Englishwoman who had refused to become his mistress but, otherwise, such marriages were unheard of for kings. Without an English love waiting in October 1537, Henry turned instead to the more conventional route of a foreign marriage.

Jane Seymour had not yet been buried when the first tentative steps were taken towards identifying her successor. Within days of her death Henry's chief minister, Thomas Cromwell, wrote to the French ambassadors suggesting that either the French king's daughter or his kinswoman, Mary of Guise might be suitable. Such haste appears indecent nowadays but, in the eyes of his contemporaries, Henry had little to be embarrassed about and the death of his wife created a vacancy that needed filling. As Cromwell wrote at the end of November 1537, the Imperial ambassadors welcomed Henry's new availability and 'upon the decease of the queen the ambassadors made an overture for the daughter of Portugal. It was thankfully taken, but would have been more so had it come anew from the Emperor, but it appears they did it upon an old commission'. At the age of forty-six, Henry VIII had suddenly become the most eligible man in Europe.

By the end of 1537 ambassadors had been instructed to search the courts of Europe for a potential bride. John Hutton, Henry's ambassador to Mary of Hungary, Regent of the Netherlands, provided one of the earliest reports, writing to Cromwell from Brussels that he had made a secret search of the eligible ladies in the area. According to Hutton:

> There is in the Court waiting upon the queen the daughter of the lord of Breidroot, 14 years old and of goodly stature, virtuous, sad and womanly. Her mother, who is dead, was daughter to the cardinal of Luike's sister; and the Cardinal would give her a good dote [dowry]. There is the widow of the late earl of Egmond, who repairs often to the Court. She is over 40, but does not look it. There is the duchess of Milan, who is reported a goodly personage and of excellent beauty. The duke of Cleves has a daughter, but there is no great praise either of her personage or her beauty.

The inclusion of Anne in the list of eligible ladies was the first time that an alliance with Cleves had been suggested since 1530. Hutton's comments about her appearance seem prophetic given Henry's own later claims about her looks. However, it is very unlikely that anyone at Brussels had ever been in the same room as Anne, let alone come near enough to her to scrutinize her appearance. In any event Anne's inclusion in the list of ladies drew no comment from the king and, at the end of 1537, he had no interest in an alliance with Anne, or any of the other ladies in the list. By Christmas 1537 Henry had decided who he wanted to become his fourth bride and it was not Anne of Cleves.

In December 1537 Francis I of France wrote to Castillon, his ambassador in England, saying that it would be a great honour if Henry took a French bride and that 'there is no lady who is not at his commandment except Madame de Longueville, whose marriage with the king of Scots has been arranged'. Henry's nephew, James V of Scotland, had married Francis's daughter Madeleine early in 1537 and taken her back to Scotland with him as his queen. The cold climate affected the new Queen of Scots' already frail health and she died only weeks after arriving in her new country. This was a personal blow to both Francis and James, but it had no effect on the alliance between the two countries and Francis immediately offered James Mary of Guise, the widowed Duchess of Longueville, as a second wife.

Mary of Guise was the eldest daughter of the Duke of Guise, one of the most powerful noblemen in France. Her father was also the younger brother of the Duke of Lorraine and the uncle of Anne's proposed husband, Francis of Lorraine. Mary of Guise bore her first husband two sons during their brief marriage and, to Henry, appeared a most attractive proposition, regardless of her betrothal to his nephew. According to Castillon, by the end of December 1537, Henry's thoughts of marriage were increasingly centred on Mary of Guise:

> [The king] is so amorous of Madame de Longueville that he cannot refrain from coming back upon it. I assured him that the marriage between the king of Scots and her had already been sworn before my first letters; but that no lady in France would be denied him. He replied that he could not believe, even though her father M. de Guise had sworn and promised with M. d'Albrot (the abbot of Arbroath), that Madame de Longueville had consented to it; for when I said to him, 'would you marry another man's wife?' he said he knew well that she had not spoken, and asked me to write to you, if matters were not so far advanced that they could not be broken off, to deliver her to him, and he would do twice as much for you [Francis] as the king of Scots would.

Castillon was unable to keep Henry off the subject of the beautiful Mary of Guise and the king was smitten, arguing that 'he was big in person and had need of a big wife'. Part of Mary's attraction for Henry was the King of Scots' interest in her and he was eager to best his nephew and neighbour. He was also a romantic at heart and wanted to be in love with his wife. The unusually tall and reportedly beautiful Mary of Guise fitted the bill for Henry perfectly.

There is some evidence that Mary herself desired marriage with the uncle rather than the nephew. Henry's confidence that Mary was not yet betrothed to James was based on reliable sources and he had already sent an agent to meet with Mary privately in order to find out her own thoughts on the marriage. Mary received Peter Mewtas, the English emissary, gladly and informed him that, although her father had indeed sworn that she would marry James, she had never been asked for her consent or given it and, although she was ready to obey Francis in everything, she had never promised to marry the Scottish king. While James was considerably younger than his uncle and Mary had the advantage of having met the Scottish king, Scotland was a distant land and one rumoured to be considerably less comfortable than her home in France. Mary may also have reasoned that, if she had to leave her sons and her home to become a queen, she might as well make the more prestigious match and marry the powerful king of England. In February 1538 Henry again sent Mewtas to visit Mary, anxious to discover whether she still favoured his suit.

That Mary favoured Henry over James is also suggested by a letter written by her mother in January 1538. In this letter the Duchess of Guise lamented the fact that Mary's marriage contract with James had been drawn up, saying that 'I am afraid things will not be done so much for your advantage as I wished'. The Duchess sought to console her daughter pointing out that 'if you are in Scotland, they say the distance by sea is not long, and England is even nearer' and it is clear that both women knew that the choice was not Mary's. Francis was anxious to maintain good relations with his former son-in-law, James, and was not prepared to consider breaking an alliance when there were plenty of other suitable women for Henry to marry in France. Even Henry was forced to finally admit defeat and James V and Mary of Guise were married by proxy in May 1538.

The loss of Mary of Guise was a blow to Henry and, at first, he was not prepared to consider an alternative French bride. In a conversation with the king in May 1538, Castillon found him particularly petulant, lamenting that Francis had preferred him to the pope and the King of Scots. He did, however, perk up a little when Castillon assured him that Mary had a sister 'as beautiful and graceful clever and well fitted to please and obey him as any other'. This piqued Henry's interest and, the following day, a member of Henry's council was sent to discuss a new marriage with Castillon. The French ambassador assured him, when questioned on the ladies of France, that 'France was a warren of honourable ladies' for Henry to choose from, something that Henry took entirely literally.

On 31 May 1538 the French ambassador wrote to the French court asking for three or four candidates for Henry's marriage to be suggested. Mary of Guise's younger sister, Louise, was a likely candidate for Henry and he had received reports that she was more beautiful than her elder sister. Shortly afterwards he heard of a third Guise sister, apparently more beautiful than the others, and requested her portrait too, in spite of the fact that she was soon to become a nun. While Henry intended to take a foreign bride in order to build an alliance, he also wanted to ensure that his wife was beautiful. In July he asked his ambassador in France to suggest that three potential brides, Mesdemoiselles de Vendome, de Lorraine and de Guise should be brought to Calais chaperoned by Francis's sister so that Henry himself could select his favourite. This suggestion was met with an indignant refusal by Francis and instead the French king told Henry to send someone he trusted to survey the ladies. Henry's displeasure at this refusal was mollified somewhat when he received a portrait of Louise of Guise which he found pleasing, but he was still determined to view the ladies himself.

To modern observers, Henry's attempts to view the potential brides himself appears natural, but to Francis and the ladies themselves, it was shocking. Henry himself had resisted sending a portrait of his own daughter, Mary, during marriage negotiations for her hand, arguing that her breeding was enough to recommend her and the French took the same view when Henry's suggestion was made. Francis was scandalized, stating that the women were not horses to be made to promenade on show. The issue came to a head in August 1538 during a conversation between Henry and Castillon. Henry demanded to know whether Francis had sent him anything regarding the marriages. Castillon replied that Francis did not consider the proposed meeting in Calais honourable. To this, Henry responded: 'By God, I trust no one but myself. The thing touches me too near. I wish to see them and know them some time before deciding.' Castillon then sarcastically asked whether Henry also wanted to try out the ladies before he made his choice, causing Henry to blush in shame. This was the last time that Henry raised the suggestion of a meeting at Calais although he did later hint that if the ladies could find some pretext to stay at a house near Calais, he might come to them in disguise to make his choice.

Although Henry showed an interest in a French bride after the loss of Mary of Guise, by early 1538 his attention had already turned to an Imperial candidate. One of the ladies mentioned in John Hutton's despatch from Brussels, in which Anne was also considered, was the Duchess of Milan. The Duchess charmed Hutton upon her arrival in Brussels in December 1537 and he reported that she resembled Margaret Shelton, a former mistress of the king. For Henry, this was high praise indeed and Hutton's next report roused his interest further when the ambassador recorded that:

> there is none in these parts for beauty of person and birth to be compared to the Duchess. She is not so pure white as the late queen [Jane Seymour], whose soul God pardon, but she hath a singular countenance, and when she chanceth to smile there appeareth two pittes in her cheeks and one in her chin, the which become her right excellently well.

With the loss of Mary of Guise, the Duchess of Milan became the frontrunner for Henry's hand. Christina of Denmark, Duchess of Milan, was only fifteen when she caught Henry's interest. As the daughter of Isabella of Austria, sister of Charles V and Christian II of Denmark, she had endured a turbulent early childhood with the deposition and subsequent imprisonment of her father and the death of her mother. Christina was raised by her aunt, Mary of Hungary, in the Netherlands and became a favourite of the Regent. When, at the age of eleven, Christina had been betrothed to the thirty-eight-year-old Duke of Milan, Mary of Hungary vigorously resisted the marriage out of concern for her niece, but to no avail. Christina was sent to Milan in June 1535 where she proved an exemplary duchess and an excellent wife for her sickly husband. Her husband's death in 1537 left her once again much sought after as a bride with even Anne of Cleves' brother, William, emerging as a suitor.

After the death of her husband, Christina returned to her aunt in Brussels. Mary of Hungary had no great opinion of Henry VIII, the man who had divorced her aunt, Catherine of Aragon, and at the time of his third marriage wrote that:

> It is to be hoped – if one can hope anything from such a man – that when he is tired of this wife he will find some better way of getting rid of her. Women, I think, would hardly be pleased if such customs became general, and with good reason; and although I have no wish to expose myself to similar risks, yet, as I belong to the feminine sex, I, too, will pray that God may preserve us from such perils.

She was therefore alarmed when, in January 1538, she discovered that Henry was considering that he 'might honour the said Duchess by marriage, her virtue, qualities and behaviour being reported to be such as is worthy to be much advanced'.

In February 1538 Hutton received a formal commission to treat for Henry's marriage to Christina. As with Henry's earlier suit towards Mary of Guise, attempts were made to assess Christina's view of the marriage. In May he reported that he had been able to talk many times to Christina and that he found her both full of wisdom and modesty. She treated him kindly and gratefully accepted the present of some hounds and a horse which he gave her, thankfully telling Hutton that she had never been so well horsed before.

This was all positive for Henry's suit and, in July, Hutton was also able to report that Christina had showed an interest in England and its king when she questioned a gentleman of her household upon his return from Henry's kingdom. Christina granted a further interview to two new ambassadors sent by Henry to press his suit in October 1538 and they reported that 'she is a goodly personage of stature higher than either of us, and competently fair, but very well favoured, a little brown'. Although Christina was not a great beauty, she consistently drew favourable reports from Henry's agents and her sober demeanour was much lauded. She was also content to participate in the marriage negotiations and, in March 1538, supplied Hutton with a portrait of herself to send to Henry. This portrait was duly dispatched and, when the very next day Henry's painter, Hans Holbein, arrived to paint her, Christina sat for a portrait again. Holbein took a quick sketch of Christina before returning rapidly to England. The likeness enchanted Henry and he ordered a full portrait to be painted. It is clear, from the portrait, that Christina was pleasing enough, dressed in deepest mourning. Her face showed her Habsburg ancestry with her strong jaw. Upon receipt of the portrait, Henry ordered musicians to play for him and for a time the court was the scene of festivities as the king contemplated his fourth marriage.

While Christina was willing to participate in the marriage negotiations, there is some indication that she was not entirely happy with the suit of the aged king. One contemporary, George Constantine, had heard, by the summer of 1539, that Christina had required a pledge for her own safety from the king before embarking on matrimony with him. According to Constantine,

> she sayeth that the Kynges maiestie was in so little space rydde of the Quenes, that she dare not trust his cownceill, though she durst trust his maiestie. For her cownceill suspecteth that her great Aunt [Catherine of Aragon] was poisoned; that the second [Anne Boleyn] was innocentlye put to deeth; and the therd [Jane Seymour] lost for lacke of kepinge in her child bed.

Christina is also traditionally supposed to have responded to Henry's proposal with the comment that 'she had but one head, if she had two, one should be at his Majesty's service'. It is unlikely Christina ever made a comment as indiscreet as this, but she may have thought it. The most enthusiastic comment that the English ambassadors could draw from her was 'as for mine inclination, what should I say? You know I am at the Emperor's commandment'.

Henry first declared his interest in Christina early in 1538 and, by spring, negotiations were well under way. In April 1538 Henry's commissioners sat down to negotiate both Henry's marriage and the marriage of his daughter, Princess Mary, to the emperor's kinsman, Dom Luis of Portugal. During the negotiations, Henry was offered a dowry of 100,000 crowns from the emperor in money and 15,000 crowns in yearly rent. In return he guaranteed that there would be titles and revenue enough for the sons that Christina would bear him, optimistically naming the dukedoms of York, Gloucester and Somerset for his younger sons. While negotiations initially went well, they soon became bogged down with Henry insisting that Charles V guarantee Christina's revenue from the duchy of Milan in the event that it should be seized by the French. Henry also insisted that Christina's elder sister abandon her own rights to the throne of Denmark in favour of her younger sister. Henry then complained that, while in normal circumstances the family of the bride would pay for their journey to their new country, Christina's journey from Brussels would be considerably shorter, and less expensive, than Mary's journey to Portugal. The Imperial ambassadors countered that Mary's dowry was too small and, in return, Henry argued that the dower offered to his daughter, in the event that her husband pre-deceased her, would not be enough to support her.

The negotiations in England were hindered by the distance between England and Spain and the need for Charles V to be consulted on the finer points of the negotiations. In recognition of this, on 26 July 1538 Charles V granted a commission to his sister, Mary of Hungary, to negotiate Christina's marriage. The Queen Regent was far from happy with the match suggested for her pretty young niece and she quickly found that her brother, the emperor, was not entirely certain that the marriage was in his best interests. Francis I and Charles V had spent much of the past twenty years in continual war, something which had often worked to Henry's advantage as both sides sought to make alliances with him against the other. However, in early 1538, the two powers' foreign policy suddenly changed and the emperor and the French king decided to make an alliance. In summer 1538 Francis was persuaded to meet the pope and, while he refused to see the emperor there, a peace was brokered between the two former enemies. The two rulers then met at the town of Aigues-Mortes in France. This was a major turning point for their relations and, soon afterwards, the Emperor and the French king concluded an agreement for a permanent peace.

The news of the friendship between Francis and Charles was greeted with both anger and fear in England and Henry increased his attempts to arrange a marriage with Christina. In June 1538 Hutton wrote to England to report that he had secured an interview with Mary of Hungary shortly after her return from a hunting trip with Christina. According to Hutton, he complained to the regent that:

> The Emperor, who had made the first overtures touching the duchess of Milan, had now become so cold, that his ambassadors in England had no instructions to conclude anything, and that he was sorry for it, as he had hoped that such an alliance would revive the old friendship between England and the house of Burgundy.

The regent promised to use her influence with her brother but she was unenthusiastic and by late in 1538 the English ambassadors to Brussels were complaining that she had turned cold towards them. Mary had herself met with the French king as part of the Imperial-French alliance in October and, in all probability, her cold demeanour towards the English ambassadors was based on the hope that the problem that they represented would just go away. Henry was determined to put pressure upon the regent and, in September, his ambassadors were instructed to press her for a final decision. Mary was at a loss as to how to respond and, by January 1539 she was writing to her brother saying: 'I beg you once more, Monseigneur, to tell me if I am to keep these negotiations dragging on, for I can no longer do this without the most shameless hypocrisy.'

By January 1539 it was clear to everyone that no marriage between Henry and Christina would be made. It was also obvious that no new French marriage would be suggested. On 12 January 1539 Charles and Francis signed the treaty of Toledo in which they promised to make no new agreements with Henry without the other's express consent. Already, in December 1538, the pope had proclaimed that the original Bull of Excommunication against Henry, frozen since its issue in 1535, would be brought into force and, soon after Christmas, he sent Henry's hated cousin, Cardinal Pole, to the emperor and the French king with the view of persuading them to mount a holy war against the schismatic king. When Henry also received word that the emperor and the French king intended to withdraw their ambassadors in England both he, and the country as a whole, became deeply alarmed. In the light of these events Henry and his chief minister, Thomas Cromwell, looked around desperately for a new marriage alliance to strengthen the king's position. By early January 1539 their attention had turned towards Anne of Cleves.

3

The Noblest & Highest Honour:
January 1539 – October 1539

Henry's marriage negotiations with Christina of Milan continued well into 1539 but, with the treaty of Toledo in January of that year, it was clear to everyone that the marriage would never be finalized. As a widower, Henry's marriage was, along with his daughter Mary's, one of the greatest assets that England had and the country was badly in need of allies.

The friendship between Francis I of France and the Emperor Charles V fuelled a growing paranoia in England with the country alert to the threat of invasion. Henry set about preparing England for the possible invasion and he 'caused all the havens to be fortefyed and roads to Dover, and caused bulwarkes to be made on the sea coastes, and sent commissions throughout all the realm, to have his people muster'. The atmosphere throughout the early months of 1539 was tense with the slightest rumour, such as a report of unknown ships lying off the coast at Easter, bringing people to arms. In May 1539 Henry personally viewed a muster of the men of the city of London and he sent commissioners throughout England to have the people ready themselves with arms.

The king's chief minister, Thomas Cromwell, had come to prominence during Henry's divorce from Catherine of Aragon. While there is some debate about the nature of Cromwell's religious beliefs and personal politics, he was perceived to be sympathetic towards the religious reform movement. He was also interested in building links with the Schmalkaldic League and, as the friendship between Francis and Charles grew, Henry also came to look towards Germany.

As early as 1531 the Schmalkaldic League had considered building an alliance with England and sent ambassadors to Henry. Henry's response was lukewarm but, in 1533, he sent ambassadors both to Bavaria and Saxony in an attempt to open relations. This embassy met with little success and in July 1535 Henry despatched Robert Barnes, a known religious reformer and associate of Cromwell, to Germany in order to arrange for Philip Melanchthon, a leading Lutheran theologian, to come to England. Neither Anne's brother-in-law, John Frederick of Saxony, nor Philip, Landgrave of Hesse, were prepared to send Melanchthon, their leading theologian. However, in March 1538 they did consent to sent an embassy headed by Georg von Boineburg, a Hessian diplomat, and Franz Burchard, John Frederick's vice-chancellor. The main purpose of this embassy was to discover the religious differences between England and the League and perhaps to prepare for England's admission to the Schmalkaldic League. In England the ambassadors conferred and debated with Henry's own theologians for some months arguing strongly that 'three heads of papal idolatry must be got rid of if the power of Rome is to be rooted out: the prohibition of communion in both kinds, private masses and enforced clerical celibacy'. Unbeknown to the ambassadors, these were requirements with which Henry could never agree but the embassy was a success and, on 1 October 1538, Henry wrote to John Frederick requesting that Melanchton be sent to him next time for further discussions.

While Henry's interest in Germany had always been lukewarm, the success of the League's embassy to England and the dangerous political situation in Europe caused him to increase his efforts to woo Germany by January 1539. It is certain that Cromwell helped to push the king towards the League but, equally, Henry was able to see the wisdom of an approach to the leading anti-Imperial power in Europe. In January 1539 Henry decided to send his own embassy, appointing Christopher Mont, a German-born member of Cromwell's household, as his ambassador. Henry set out detailed instructions to his ambassador, ordering him to go to John Frederick and question him on 'the inclination which both dukes of Cleves, father and son, bear to the bishop of Rome [the pope]; he shall enquire, in case they are still of the old popish fashion, whether they will be inclinable to alter their opinions'. Henry's interest in Cleves is explained in further instructions given to Mont by Cromwell. Mont was to speak to Burchard about a possible marriage to be arranged between Princess Mary, Henry's eldest daughter, and Anne of Cleves' brother, William. Once this had been discussed he was to:

> Diligently but secretly inquere of the beautie and qualities of the lady eldest of booth doughters to the duke of Cleves, as well what shape, stature, proportion and complexion she is of as of her lerning actyvitie, bihauiour and honest qualities. And if the said Christopher Mont shall heare, that she is such as might be likened vnto his Maiestie then he shall say unto the said Burgartus that the lorde Cromwell muche tendering the kinge's alliaunce in Germany, if he could fynde any occasion wolbe glad to employe himself earnestly to induce and persuade the kinges hieghnes his souerain lorde rather to joyn with them then otherwise, specially for the duke of Saxonyes sake who is allyed ther, and to make a crosse maryage bitwen the young duke of Cleves and my lady Mary as is aforesaid. And of the kinges hienes with the said elder doughter of Cleves.

Mont was instructed to hint at the marriage but 'nevetheles not as demaunding her, but as giving them a prick to stir them to offer her, as the noblest, and hieghest honour that could come unto that noble house of Cleves, if they could bring it to passe'.

Cromwell's instructions to Mont are the first indication that Anne was considered as a potential bride since her name had been mentioned in passing by Henry's ambassador in Brussels at the end of 1537. While Cleves was not a member of the Schmalkaldic League, Anne's position, as the sister-in-law of John Frederick, made her the most eligible bride that the League had. John Frederick was willing to consider the marriage of his sister-in-law, and, at a meeting with Mont, promised to do all he could to advance 'this honest affair'. He also promised to send a picture of Anne although, unfortunately, there would be a delay as his painter was sick at home. This news was a blow to Henry and his chief minister, but Mont was able to reassure them both that 'everyone praises the lady's beauty, both of face and body. One said she excelled the Duchess [of Milan] as the golden sun did the silver moon'. Mont had, of course, never seen Anne, but the reports of those that had were encouraging and Henry, at the urging of Cromwell, was determined to press his suit.

By January 1539 Anne's brother, William, had taken possession of Guelders, but he was still unable to persuade the emperor to recognize his claim and the duchy was a source of conflict between him and Charles. The mood of the court at Cleves was further darkened on 6 February 1539 with the death of Anne's father, John III. Anne spent her childhood closely supervised by her mother, and her father was a distant figure in her life. Nonetheless, his death was a shock to her and highlighted the passing of time and the fact that, by early 1539, she was in her early twenties with no concrete marriage plans arranged for her.

While the death of John III was a personal blow for Anne, it did nothing to reduce the sudden interest shown in her by Henry. On 10 March 1539 Henry drafted instructions for an embassy to be sent to Cleves, requesting that they should first inquire into Anne's appearance and character and 'knowing her to be such as is not to be misliked, ye shall require access unto the said Duke'. The ambassadors were instructed to offer friendship to William and to request a sight of Anne. They were also to inform William that, providing Henry liked Anne, he 'will be glad to honour his house and family with matrimony with her and to depart as liberally with her and with so convenient conditions as he shall have cause to be contented'. That same day Cromwell also wrote to inform Mont and his colleague, Thomas Paynell, that Henry had decided to send ambassadors to Cleves as the behaviour of Mary of Hungary towards the proposed marriage of Christina of Milan had grown so cold that it could be taken as practically a refusal.

The English ambassadors, led by Nicholas Wotton, were greeted favourably in Cleves and they immediately set out to try to obtain a portrait of Anne. Anne and her younger sister, Amelia, were in evidence at court and the English ambassadors were permitted to see them from the first, if only distantly. As Wotton and his fellow ambassador, Richard

Berde, complained in May when he was offered pictures of both sisters by Dr Henry Olisleger, vice-chancellor of Cleves: '[And for a]s muche as we hadde not seene the ij ladyes, we shulde [not be] able to advertise his Majestye whether theyr imaiges wer [l]yke to theyr persones, and so shulde his Majestye be never the nerre by the sight of the pictures'. Olisleger replied that he could assure the king of the accuracy of the portraits but, as the ambassadors pointed out, they were having difficulty getting a clear sight of the two princesses as 'we sayde, we hadde not seene theym, for to see but a parte of theyr faces, and that under such monstruouse habyte and apparel, was no sight, neither of they[r] faces nor of theyr persones'. This complaint fell on deaf ears in Cleves with Olisleger replying sarcastically: 'why, wolde you see theym nakydde?' Olisleger eventually promised them a closer view of both princesses but neither was expected to play more than a distant role in affairs.

Towards the end of April Cromwell was able to report to Henry that John Frederick had exhorted William to go through with the proposed marriage for Anne and that he had sent ambassadors to his brother-in-law in Cleves. It was a flattering offer for Anne and her brother, but in the early months of 1539 William was still not entirely convinced that an alliance with Henry would be advantageous. In April and May 1539 rumours reached England that William was hoping to negotiate with the emperor, with the possibility of even marrying the Duchess of Milan himself. This was not what either Henry or Cromwell wanted to hear and Henry instructed his ambassadors to force William to give his opinion of the match.

On 30 April Wotton and Berde were finally offered an audience with William at the town of Cleves, with an appointment to arrive at 8 o'clock in the morning. The ambassadors waited all day but heard nothing until the evening when one of William's secretaries came to them and requested that they make themselves available the next day. The next day Olisleger came to the ambassadors and told them that the:

Beste of his company came hither the day before somewhat late, [wh]ich was the cause that we had not been spoken withal that day, and that they, who were the Chancellor Hograve, and the Marshall and certain other, had brought him letters from the Duke and also showed him by mouth that he, the said Chancellor Olisleger, should in the Duke's name give us this answer. That the Duke considered very well how much he was bound to the king and was sorry he could not answer him so shortly as he would, having been disappointed of an opportunity of conference with the duke of Saxony.

Olisleger reported that William was anxious for more information about the proposed terms of the marriage and that nothing could be concluded until he had received this. Olisleger also surprised the ambassadors by offering Amelia's portrait as well as Anne's.

Anne, as the eldest unmarried sister, had always been the focus of Henry's interest due to the more favourable inheritance rights that she would have if William and Sibylla died without issue. The ambassadors thanked Olisleger for the offer of Amelia's portrait but continued to persist in their attempts to get William to commit to the marriage with Anne. Upon further pressure being applied, Olisleger finally admitted the true cause of the delays and William's desire to consult with John Frederick. According to the ambassadors, Olisleger said:

And as for the lady Anne, he sayde, as to his frendis secretelye, that the old Duke of Cleves and the Duke of Lorayne hadde ben yn communicacion together for the mariaige of the Marquyse, the duke of Loraynes sonne, and the said ladye Anne, and that they hadde gone so ferre that wrytinges wer made and sealyd up on hit, and that the duke of Cleves hadde payed thereupon to the duke of Gheldres by the said agreement certeyn sommes of money, and hadde fulfilled on his part all things, saving that the lady Anne was not yet maryed to the said Marquyse. Why then, quod we, it is but yn vayne to speake enye more of my ladye Anne, for she is fast ynnough ensueryd all redye. Naye, quod the Chawncelour, not so, for these promises wer made onelye betwixt the fathers, and the parties as yet have not given theyr consentes, but ar at theyr libertye to do what they wille.

Upon receiving the assurance that Anne was free to marry, the ambassadors again pressed Olisleger for an answer. Olisleger continued to insist that a conference with John Frederick was necessary. In the light of this, the ambassadors were left with the suspicion of some underhand dealing by William, noting that Anne's brother need not press too hard for her marriage to either Francis of Lorraine or Henry VIII as 'he knowithe well ynnough that her beawtye wille g[et her] a goode husbande'.

The news of Anne's betrothal to Francis of Lorraine was a major blow to Henry's hopes of the marriage and everything hinged on whether or not it had been truly broken off, leaving her free to marry. In July Henry sent a further ambassador, Dr Peter, to Cleves in an attempt to find out the true position. Recognizing that Anne's mother was the person most likely to know the progress of negotiations, the king ordered his ambassadors to seek out Maria of Juliers and 'using all their wisdom and d[exterity] to kindle them to desire of this matter, specia[lly in] their conferences with the Duchess, labouring therein as much as they may to allure and get her to be earnest in th[e deter]mination and speedy conclusion of the same'. He was to flatter the Duchess and then mention Anne's betrothal to both William and his mother, focussing especially on the Duchess, and asking them to 'open the bottom of their stomachs' concerning the matter. Henry ordered Peter to view the papers concerning the agreement with Lorraine but that, in the event that the Duchess did indeed confess that Anne was promised but that Amelia was free, they were to say that 'all should be one to the king, but that as his Grace preferred the eldest they must refer again to him'.

While Henry instructed his ambassadors to report to him on Anne's appearance, he was not prepared to rely on their word alone and, in the summer of 1539, he dispatched his court painter, Hans Holbein, to Cleves to paint both Anne and Amelia. The sisters had previously sat for a portrait a year before. However, both sisters viewed the arrival of the artist with excitement and Anne was well aware that she was the true focus of the English embassy's interest. She also came into closer contact with the English ambassadors and Nicholas Wotton was able to provide details of Anne's education and character to the king. Upon seeing the portraits he was also able to declare that Holbein 'hathe expressyd theyr imaiges verye lyvelye' and that the portraits were considered a good likeness by those who had seen Anne and Amelia.

The portraits were rushed back to England for the approval of the king. Amelia's portrait has not survived but the image of Anne still exists. Anne's portrait shows her standing facing the artist wearing rich and heavy clothes in the German style and, to modern eyes, it is pleasing. Henry's reaction to the portrait is not recorded but it must have been favourable and he continued in his determination to marry Anne. Wotton's letter, written to accompany the portrait, also pleased the king and he was able to report: 'I fynd the Counsell willing yn nough to publisshe and manifeste to the world, that by eny covenauntes made by th'olde Duke of Cleves and the Duke of Lorayne, my Lady Anne is not bownden; but ever hath ben and yet is at her free libertye to marye where ever she wille.' This was a good enough assurance for the king and he continued in his pursuit of Anne rather than Amelia.

While Anne, like her brother, remained a Catholic, the marriage was viewed positively by Protestants in both England and Germany. John Frederick hoped that it would lead Henry towards a greater interest in the religious reform and, certainly, many of Henry's actions over the past six years encouraged him in this belief. In 1533, for example, in order to divorce Catherine of Aragon, the emperor's aunt, Henry had declared himself head of the Church of England in place of the pope. The dissolution of the monasteries in England, which began in 1536, was further evidence of Henry's commitment to reform, as were injunctions sent by Cromwell in September 1538 to all bishops and curates in England. These declared that all parish churches should provide the Bible in English and that wax tapers should be removed from churches.

John Frederick was interested in the reforms and wrote to Henry asking him to accept the religious principals of the Schmalkaldic League as made 'against the ungodly religion and tyranny of the Bishop of Rome'. John Frederick continued that:

Your royal Majesty doth well remember, how diligently, before this time, you have treated with us by ambassadors, orators, and letters, to make a league in the cause of religion, and have advertised us to constancy in the defence enterprised of true religion. And this last year the orators of your regal Majesty entreated with us in the Council of Frankford of the same matter, that we should send our orators with commandments to make a league with the defence of true religion, against the tyranny of the Bishop of Rome, and not of any other causes.

Anyone who believed that Henry had embraced the religious reform was destined to be disappointed and his behaviour in the summer of 1539 left them 'astonished'.

In spite of the hopes of John Frederick and the German Protestants, Henry VIII never had any intention of bringing about a full Protestant reformation in England. Henry shared some of his beliefs with the reformers but other elements of his faith remained resolutely conservative and, in June 1539, this was demonstrated with the passage of the Act of the Six Articles. The Act was only passed with a great deal of personal pressure on parliament and the bishops from Henry and it was a statement of the king's desire to protect traditional values. The Act stated that:

Where the king's most excellent Majesty is, by God's law, Supreme Head immediately under him of this whole church and congregation of England, intending the conservation of this same church and congregation in a true, sincere and uniform doctrine of Christ's religion, calling also to his most blessed and gracious remembrance as well and great and quiet assurance, prosperous increase and other innumerable commodities, which have ever ensued, come and followed, of concord, agreement and unity in opinions, as also the manifold perils, dangers and inconveniences which have heretofore, in many places and regions, grown, sprung and arisen, of the diversities of minds and opinions especially of matters of Christian religion, and therefore desiring that such a unity might and should be charitably established in all things touching and concerning the same.

The Act set out six articles of faith to which the king expected everyone to adhere, expressly rejecting Protestant ideas such as the marriage of priests and affirming the miracle of the Eucharist. It also laid down the penalty of death for offences under the Act, earning it the nicknames among reformers of 'the whip wyth syxe strynges' and 'the bloudy statute'. The Act had a detrimental effect on the marriage negotiations and John Frederick, who had hitherto been in favour of the match, quickly became opposed to it, writing that he thought that Cleves would have 'little joy or favour with it'. As a contemporary Englishman, George Constantine commented, with accuracy: 'How can the Germaynes be our frendes, when we conclude them heretiques in our actes of Parleamente.'

The Act damaged Henry's hopes of an alliance with the League but, by August 1539, his negotiations with Cleves were already far advanced. On 18 September an embassy headed by Burchard, who had been sent by John Frederick only with the greatest reluctance, arrived in London. He was accompanied by Olisleger and other ambassadors from Cleves and Saxony and the embassy was conducted to Windsor by the Earl of Sussex. Henry was eager to please the men and for eight days they were entertained with feasting, hunting and other pleasures before the real business began. The ambassadors found Henry in good form and, while upon their arrival he was ill with a cold, within days he was out hunting with the ladies of his court, eagerly anticipating his coming marriage. The French ambassador also commented that Henry 'is in very good health, being as active and joyous as his ministers ever saw him'.

The list of the items to be discussed in the negotiations for Anne's marriage survives. The commissioners were empowered by Henry to negotiate on the dowry he would require and the lands and income that Anne would receive. The number of lords and other attendants to accompany Anne was also discussed, as were the preparations for Anne's journey and arrival. William's ambassadors asked that Anne be given the dower that her predecessors had received, something that was readily granted. The dowry that William would pay to Henry was more problematic and his ambassadors admitted that their master could not 'offer what they think convenient; for they could never pay it, the Duke being a young prince newly [come] to his dominions and forced to pronounce daily against his enemies'. William's poverty had already been anticipated by the king and, while it was agreed that Anne's brother would provide her with a dowry of 100,000 florins, a further agreement confirmed that Henry did not expect the sum to be paid. Provision for Anne's future children was discussed, as was Anne's financial position in the event that she was widowed.

By the end of September the marriage treaty had been agreed. It was favourable to Anne, granting her a dower of 20,000 gold florins if she remained in England during her widowhood. In a provision that would, in her later life, look very attractive to Anne, she was also granted an annual pension of 15,000 florins in the event that she was childless and wanted to return home to Cleves in her widowhood, as well as being able to retain her jewels and clothes, although this pension could be redeemed by Henry's heirs for a payment of 150,000 florins if they so wished. These provisions would have assured Anne a comfortable widowhood, necessary given the age difference between her and the king. Anne's succession rights were also guaranteed in the event that William and Sibylla both died without heirs. John Frederick also covenanted to pay both Anne and Amelia 100,000 florins if Sibylla inherited William's lands.

The German ambassadors returned swiftly to Cleves where William ratified the treaty. Shortly after this Anne was informed that she was to leave her home. By the signature of the marriage treaty, Anne's brother had agreed for her to marry the King of England, regardless of her own personal feelings in the matter. To Anne, the conclusion of negotiations was both terrifying and exciting and she immediately set about her preparations to leave her home and marry one of the most notorious husbands in history.

4
Conveyed by Land:
October 1539 – December 1539

With the ratification of the marriage treaty, Henry was anxious for his bride to join him in England and, with winter approaching, both Anne and her mother knew that they had only a limited time in which to make preparations. For Anne, the thought of leaving her home must have been daunting; at twenty-four years old, she had never spent any length of time away from her mother and her younger sister. She was also aware that she was unlikely to see her family ever again.

England was indeed very distant from Cleves and the journey, in winter, daunted even the most seasoned of travellers. The most direct, and usual, route was for travellers to make their way overland through the Low Countries and into Calais before taking a short sea voyage to Dover. With the Low Countries ruled by Charles V's sister, Mary of Hungary, both Henry and his advisers were concerned that a safe-conduct for Anne might not be granted, leaving it impossible for her to travel to England by land. This was a particular concern to both Henry and William and the pope himself recommended that safe-conduct should not be granted if rumours that Anne was a Lutheran were proved to be correct. Alternatively, and even more alarmingly, there was the danger that war could break out during Anne's journey, leaving her stranded and in danger as she crossed hostile territory. For Henry, the solution was obvious even before the marriage treaty. Henry had spent a great deal of money on building his navy and the idea of using his fleet to sail across hostile waters to rescue his bride from the hands of the emperor fired his imagination. Juliers-Cleves had only acquired a sea port with the acquisition of Guelders and had little in the way of ships or naval knowledge but, for Henry, the possibility of his own fleet carrying Anne on the long sea voyage across the Zuider Zee and along the coast of Europe was impossibly romantic.

The main difficulty with the plan, from Henry's perspective, was the fact that no one in England had made the voyage before and there were no sailing directions for his navy to follow. The Zuider Zee was renowned for its dangerous sandbanks and the last thing Henry wanted was for his prized fleet to limp into Harderwijk, the main port of Guelders. He therefore secretly sent two experienced shipmasters, Richard Couche and John Aborough, to Guelders with instructions to produce a pilot's chart and seaman's rutter (book of sailing instructions) to be used to convey Anne to England. The expedition left several weeks before the marriage treaty was signed, arriving back in early October with the necessary directions. The rutter produced by the two men is one of the earliest surviving in England and shows the perils that could be expected from the journey. According to the rutter: 'Hardewijk standeth in the midst of the land of Geldres, upon the sea side, so that the sea breaketh against the walls of the town continually, and at the bridge without is 3 foot water at low water, which bridge is the way in to the town gate.' From the town gate, the fleet needed to follow the road and then 'from the town road a gunshot westnorwest from the sea gate is 10 foot water, and is soft black ooze and there hence you shall run off in the same course 5 or 6 miles ere you get 3 fathom water'. Worryingly 'the deepest water that is betwixt Harddyerwek and Ankcewson is 3 fathoms (or) 19 foot water and in the channel is ooze and in both sides, as well in Holland side as in Geddyres. When you be nearer the coast you shall have sand, but no good ship may come so near'.

The prospect of such a voyage in winter was terrifying and Anne had never even seen the sea. For Henry, the practical considerations paled into insignificance besides the romantic ideal of the voyage but, during the negotiations for the marriage treaty, William's ambassadors absolutely refused to consider the enterprise. According to a report of the negotiations:

They think it rather expedient to have her conveyed by land than by water; for she is young and beautiful, and if she should be transported by the seas, they fear lest the time of year being now cold and tempestuous she might there, though she were never so well ordered, take such cold or other disease, considering she was never before upon the seas, as should be to her great peril and the king's Majesty's great displeasure.

The ambassadors also complained of the danger of an attack from the Low Countries while they were at sea and they were concerned that Anne might be captured without a safe conduct. They were adamant that Henry should obtain a safe conduct as 'they think the Emperor's people would never break their safe conduct both because of the dishonour and because it would make the king, the elector of Saxe, the duke of Cleves, and all the princes of Germany their mortal enemies'. Henry persisted with the idea of the voyage but finally agreed a compromise. In the event that safe conduct could be obtained, then William would pay for his sister to travel across Europe to Calais where she would take ship to England. If safe conduct was not granted, William would send Anne to a seaport in order for her to sail to England in a 'suitable convoy of ships'.

For Henry, the attractions of the voyage began to diminish when he considered the effect that it might have on Anne's health and beauty. He reluctantly contacted Charles V for a safe conduct, quickly obtaining a favourable answer. At the end of October Henry wrote to Mary of Hungary, informing her of Charles's consent and continuing:

Begging you, most excellent Princess, Our dearest and most beloved sister and good cousin, that, taking into consideration the purport of the Emperor's letter, as well as Our own desire, as expressed in Our last letter – and, if necessary, reproduced by Our ambassadors residing at your court, or by one of them – you may be pleased, for the personal security and comfort of the said lady [Anne] and suite, to add to her passport such full orders and favourable commendations as may be required and it is in your power to give since such is, as We can see, the good intention of our said brother, the Emperor.

In spite of Charles's animosity towards both William and Henry, he was never likely to order an attack on Anne and her train. Henry's concern that Anne should be comfortable on her journey is touching and, by the time that the marriage treaty was signed, he had worked himself up into a fervour of excitement at the prospect of his bride.

For all his poor reputation as a husband, Henry was a man who liked to be married and, as with Christina of Milan, he believed himself already in love simply from seeing Anne's portrait and reading reports of her. In the last few months of 1539 he impatiently awaited the arrival of his beautiful young bride. After two years without a wife he was excited and he threw himself into the preparations for Anne's arrival.

As soon as Anne's journey was agreed, Henry ordered that ten of his finest ships be equipped in order to transport her from Calais 'in all solemnity and triumph'. Although no official announcement of the marriage had been made, by early October, Marillac the French ambassador had guessed that the marriage was already concluded and commented in his dispatch of 3 October that 'repairs and ornaments have been renewed in the king's principal house, and especially in the quarter where queens are lodged, and some of the principal lords of this court have bought much cloth of gold and silk, a thing unusual for them except for some great solemnity'. Craftsmen were kept so busy with orders placed on behalf of the king in preparation for Anne that the London agent of Lady Lisle wrote to her to complain: 'I cannot get from the gilders the head and plate of your new saddle. The business is such that is in hand for the king's highness and the queen's grace that there is much difficulty made about the same, yet have I paid for it beforehand.' Henry also spoke of his own reasons for the marriage with Marillac, informing him that he felt the marriage was a good alliance and:

That he has long desired this league with the German princes, especially with the duke of Saxony, who has married one of the sisters of the duke of Cleves, and consequently with all his confederates, among whom he expects to be able to help his friends and neighbours with as many Germans as they like to aid them, and prevent almost any serving against those whom he intends to aid. The second advantage he expects from it is prompt succour from Germany if he should be attacked, by creating a diversion on that side. The third advantage is in religion; as he hopes by the intercession of Cleves to soften many innovations in Germany, which are too harsh, and to find some middle way to compose difficulties. A fourth motive has been his desire of issue (as he has only one male child), which he could not better have than with the said lady, who is of convenient age, healthy temperament, elegant stature, and endowed with other graces, as the said king affirms.

Henry was anxious for Anne to arrive as soon as possible so that they could begin their married life together.

As well as ensuring that repairs were made at his palaces, Henry also ordered that preparations were made at all the towns along the route to London that Anne would pass through, requiring a magnificent entry at every stop in order to display both English magnificence and the joy that was felt at Anne's arrival. The most important preparations were made in Calais, which was to be Anne's first sight of English territory and both Henry and Cromwell were determined that she should be suitably impressed. In a letter of 18 October written by Cromwell to Lord Lisle, Henry's governor at Calais, the minister reported that:

The king's Majesty's pleasure is that you shall view his Grace's house here called the Exchequer, that with all diligence all things therein necessary to be amended may be undelayedly repaired. For the which purpose I have by his Grace's commandment written also to his Highness's Surveyor there, who by your advice shall set in hand the same. Furthermore, his Majesty would that you should cause the streets and lanes there to be viewed for the pavements, and where any default is, to give commandment to those which should repair the same to see it immediately amended, endeavouring yourselves to put all other things within the said town in the most honest and cleanly order you can devise; where in you shall administer to his Majesty very thankful pleasure.

Henry had not visited Calais since winter 1532 and considerable work was required on both the town and his house there to ensure that it was suitable for Anne. A schedule of the works carried out at Calais between October and December 1539 survives and shows that work continued right up to the moment when Anne arrived. This included preparing rails for the tiltyard and the Lantern Gate, which was the main gate into the city. The walls were repaired and roads re-paved. Henry's house, the Exchequer, was substantially repaired with new windows fitted and gutters replaced. Decorative work was required and royal emblems were painted and gilded over the Lantern Gate, and Henry's arms set into windows. Floors and furniture were repaired at the Exchequer and the need for twelve labourers to be paid for 'bearing away rubbish, dust, and other filth out of the exchequer' hints at the scale of the work needed to make the house habitable. Cromwell also busied himself with the appointment of officers to meet Anne at Calais and her reception committee was present in the town by the beginning of December.

From the moment that the marriage treaty was signed Anne found herself the centre of attention, even receiving a personal letter of congratulations from Cromwell himself. She also received a gift from Lady Lisle, given to Olisleger to pass on to Anne, when he passed through Calais, a gift which the ambassador reported that Anne 'taketh much pleasure. And how very acceptable that the said gift hath been to her'. Anne had little knowledge of England and, with her limited education, is unlikely to have even known where her new home was. Henry anticipated this difficulty and, early in October 1539, sent a gentlewoman, Mistress Gilmyn, to Cleves in order to become one of Anne's ladies and, presumably, instruct her in English customs. It is also likely that Mistress Gilmyn was able to teach Anne some English and to tell her about her new country and husband.

Henry was anxious to ensure that Anne's transition from German princess to English queen would be a success and Cromwell enquired on his behalf about German customs that would make Anne feel more at home when she finally arrived. According to a dispatch from Nicholas Wotton on 4 December, he enquired about a custom called 'bruidstuckes' which both Cromwell and the king were interested in. According to Wotton's informants:

The morning after marriage, a lord or great man gives his wife a *morgengave*, the value at his pleasure. Mons. de Bure gave his lady the value of 1000 francs. He also gives for *bruidstuckes* to the gentlewomen, proper rings or brooches, and to the men, doublets or jackets of velvet or silk, or velvet gowns. These gifts are to those who do service about the feast at the marriage, and to the rest, it is at his pleasure. Mr Vaughan enquired of one Harman, a merchant of the Company, who says that *bruidstucks* are only given by the lord to his own servants, and by the lady to hers; to the men caps or doublets, jackets or gowns, and chains to some; and to the women garlands, little rings or brooches. This is what the elector of Saxe did when he married the lady Sybil, and the landgrave when he married Duke Georg's daughter.

Henry almost certainly ensured that there were *bruidstucks* ready for the morning after his own wedding when Anne finally arrived.

Anne spent her last few weeks in Cleves with her mother and Amelia, preparing the clothes and other necessities that she would require for her new life in England. She received an entire new wardrobe of rich clothes, all cut in the German fashion. Preparations in Cleves took longer than expected while Henry waited impatiently for his bride in England. Anne was eagerly expected by the English court and, even in late October, John Husee wrote to Lord Lisle from the court that 'there are no other news, but men looketh for the coming of the queen, but no man knoweth the time certain'. Everyone at court had felt the lack of a queen over the previous two years and Anne Basset, one of Anne's appointed ladies in England, wrote: 'I trust to God that we shall have a mistress shortly.' Finally, towards the end of November Henry sent a courier to Cleves to learn when Anne would depart, receiving the favourable response that she would be in Calais on 8 December. For Henry, the last few months of 1539 were a time of impatience as he waited for his new bride. For Anne, however, they were the last few precious weeks at home with her family.

The date of departure finally arrived. Anne must have said a tearful farewell to her mother, sister and brother before settling into the fine chariot that had been prepared for her journey. Anne was well wrapped up against the cold and it was a comfort to her that her train was full of familiar faces. In spite of his poverty, William was determined to transport his sister to England in style and Anne left Cleves accompanied by a train of 263 people, including the Earls of Overstein and Nuennare and Dr Olisleger. Mistress Gilmyn travelled with Anne along with Lady Keteler and twelve other ladies and gentlewomen, all intended to keep Anne company. Anne's young cousin, Count von Waldeck, was also present. There were numerous servants and John Frederick had lent Anne thirteen trumpeters to proclaim her arrival in the towns along the route.

The wintery conditions and the large size of Anne's train made progress slow and they travelled only, on average, five miles a day. For Anne, who had never left Juliers-Cleves, everything seemed impossibly new but she took the rigours of the journey in good spirits. On 3 December Anne reached Antwerp, the capital of the Low Countries. Antwerp was home to a large population of English merchants and Cromwell had given orders for the merchants to prepare the English house there for Anne's reception and to provide entertainment there. Anne's reception at Antwerp was spectacular and Wotton reported that there had never been so many people gathered in the city for any entry, even the emperor's. A feast was held in Anne's honour on her arrival and she acquitted herself well in her first official reception as Queen of England. After leaving Antwerp Anne made her way slowly to Bruges, arriving on 7 December. From Bruges, Anne travelled on to Dambrugh, Newport and then Dunkirk. At Dunkirk Anne heard a sermon that was deemed to be seditious by some members of her train, something that must have affected the mood of the train somewhat. Anne did not herself complain and, when Henry ordered an investigation into the sermon, it was deemed not to have been dangerous. Anne acquitted herself well as queen throughout the journey, earning the good reports of everyone who saw her.

Anne's train finally reached Gravelines, a few miles from Calais, on 10 December 1539. Great preparations had been made for Anne's arrival and, according to Gregory Cromwell a member of the reception committee, 'it is determynd that she shall remayne here Frydaie and Satyrdaye all daie, and vppon Sondaie, wynde and wether seruynge, take hir passage into Englande'. The noblemen and gentlemen who had crossed to Calais in anticipation of Anne's arrival had already spent some days waiting for her, entertaining themselves with feasting and running at the tilt in order to ward off boredom.

Anne's first view of English soil was intended to be spectacular. According to Holinshed's Chronicle, on 11 December:

> At the towne pike on this side Graueling, was the ladie Anne of Cleue receiued by the lord deputie of the towne of Calis [Lord Lisle], and with the speares and horsemen belonging to the retinue there. When she came within little more than a mile of the towne of Calis, she was met by the erle of Southampton high admerall of England, who had in his companie thirtie gentlemen of the kings household, as Sir Francis Brian, Sir Thomas Seimer [Seymour], and others, beside a great number of gentlemen of his owne retinue clad in blue veluet, and crimson satin, and his yeomen in damaske of the same colours. The mariners of his ship were apparelled in satin of Bridges, cotes & slops of the same colour. The lord admerall brought her into Calis by Lantern Gate. There was such a peale of ordinance shot off at hir entrie, as was maruellous to the hearers. The maior presented hir with an hundred markes in gold, the merchants of the staple with an hundred sovereigns of gold in a rich purse.

No expense was spared to ensure that Anne and her retinue were impressed and the entire town came out to welcome her. She spent her first night in her future husband's kingdom at the Exchequer, tired but pleased at how favourable her reception had been.

The Earl of Southampton, Lord Admiral of England, had been appointed by Henry to host Anne's visit to Calais and then escort her to England. The following day he showed her the ships in the harbour, prepared for her voyage. Anne cannot but have been impressed by the ships decked out with banners and streamers and, when a peal of guns was shot from them, both she and her attendants commented favourably on the sight. Anne then returned to the Exchequer where she was entertained with banquets and jousting before once again retiring to bed, aware that the following day she was due to sail to England.

Although Anne's reception was a success, the weather was a concern for Southampton and the other members of her escort. On the morning of 13 December, it was clear that she would not be able to sail that day. This was a blow and Southampton immediately put in place a rota of his sailors to watch from outside the town walls for any sign that the wind was changing. He also secured Anne's approval of a scheme where she would be ready to sail as soon as the wind was fair, something that shows Anne's helpful temperament and desire to please. Anne took the enforced stay in Calais with good grace and, on the afternoon of 13 December she asked Southampton, with Olisleger acting as interpreter, if he would teach her a card game that the king played. Anne was eager to ensure that she had something in common with the king and happily played the game of 'cent', a popular game at the English court, with Southampton. According to Southampton, she played with 'a good grace and countenance' and her demeanour pleased everyone that she met. Anne also wanted to learn more about her new country and invited Southampton and some other noblemen to dinner that evening. This was a somewhat shocking request and, in England, it was unheard of for the king and queen to eat in company. However, after being assured that it was the custom of Cleves and on Anne's continual urging, Southampton consented, bringing a number of noblemen to dine with Anne that evening. Anne once again won the favourable opinions of the English and Southampton reported to Henry that 'her manner was like a princess'.

Southampton would later claim, with the hindsight of Henry's own reaction to Anne, that 'he, upon the first sight of her, considering it was than no tyme to dispraise her there whom so many had by reports and paintings so much extolled, did, by his lettres moch prayse her, and set her forth'. There is nothing in any of Southampton's reports to indicate that he was at all concerned by Anne's manner or appearance and everyone that she met in Calais was charmed by her. Lady Lisle, who spent much time with Anne at Calais, wrote favourably of her to her daughter, as is clear from her daughter Anne Basset's response:

This shall signify your ladyship that I received your letter of Hosse, and according to the contents thereof, I have declared unto the king's Highness all things, as your ladyship willed me to do, so that his Grace took the same in right good part, accepting your good will and toward mind therein as thankfully as though your ladyship had waited on her Grace hither; pondering right well the charges that my lord and your ladyship hath lately been at, and do sustain, specially at this present time. I humbly thank your ladyship of the news you write me of her Grace, that she is so good and gentle to serve and please. It shall be no little rejoicement to us, her Grace's servants here, that shall attend daily upon her. And most comfort to the king's majesty, whose Highness is not a little desirous to have her Grace here.

There is no evidence from any of the reports of Anne at Calais that anyone noticed anything amiss.

With the wind continuing to make a sea voyage impossible, Anne was forced to spend Christmas at the Exchequer. According to a letter from Cromwell to Southampton, Henry was anxious to receive Anne in England but he took the delay in good part, ordering Southampton, 'hartely soe to chere my lady and her trayne as they may think the tyme as short as the tediousnes of it woll suffer'. For Anne, the time seemed very long indeed and it is clear that she was homesick. On 18 December, while she continued to wait for a favourable wind, a packet of letters arrived from Flanders. Anne was thrilled at the news and summoned Southampton to her, asking him to open the packet in the hope that it contained letters from home. It was a bitter blow for Anne when they were found only to contain letters to Cromwell and another minister. Anne continued to be good natured and appeared content but the lack of news from home upset her deeply, in spite of the feasts and jousts put on to keep her entertained at Calais.

Anne spent fifteen days at Calais, waiting for the wind to change. Finally, on the morning of 27 December conditions were favourable enough for Anne to make the voyage. In spite of her homesickness, Anne was pleased to finally be leaving Calais and she and her retinue swiftly made their way to the fifty ships waiting in the harbour to take them to England, sailing at around noon that day. As she watched the French coast slowly vanish into the horizon, Anne must have wondered just what awaited her in England and in the husband that she had never seen.

5

A Flanders Mare:
27 December 1539 – 2 January 1540

Anne's voyage was uneventful and she landed at Deal in Kent at around five o'clock in the afternoon of 27 December 1539. She was met there by Sir Thomas Cheyne who took her to Deal Castle to rest.

Deal Castle was a newly built castle and adequate for Anne and her retinue to refresh themselves and change their clothes. It was not however considered suitable for a longer visit and, soon after Anne's arrival, she was met by Henry's brother-in-law, the Duke of Suffolk, and his young wife, Catherine Willoughby. The Bishop of Chichester also arrived and the visitors were accompanied by a large number of knights and esquires, and ladies to welcome Anne. Although tired, Anne greeted them cordially and she allowed the visitors to take her to the more comfortable Dover Castle a short distance down the coast, arriving at 11 o'clock at night. Anne was not expecting to meet Henry until her official reception at Greenwich several days away and she was also grateful for the chance to rest the following day.

While Anne was happy with the reception given to her by the people of England, her first sight of her new home was less auspicious and the weather was appalling. Both Suffolk and Cheyne were anxious on the morning of 29 December that they would have to delay the journey and they were pleasantly surprised to find that while 'the day w[as] foule and wyndye with moch hayle' and the rain and hail blew 'contynuelly in her face' Anne was so 'desirous to make haste to the king['s Highness] that her Grace forced for no nother, which [we] perceyvyng were very gladde to set her G[race] furthwards, considering if we should h[ave] lost this day'. Travellers from Dover to London generally followed a recognized route, going from Dover to Canterbury and then on to Sittingbourne, Rochester and Dartford and, while most places along the route had a residence suitable for Anne, at Sittingbourne she was forced to stay in an inn. Suffolk and Cheyne were particularly anxious not to lose a day to the weather as, if they remained longer at Dover 'we should have had to tarry at Sittyngbourne on New Year's even and New Year's Day, which we did not think a meet place for so long or else to have remained here Tuesday night, Wednesday, and Thursday, too many days to lose'. Suffolk and Cheyne were grateful to Anne when she agreed to set out and, as in Calais, she won praise for her fortitude and obliging nature. The journey to Canterbury cannot have been pleasant and it must have been with a sinking heart that Anne realized she was expected to sit through another expansive welcome in the rain and hail before she was allowed to enter her lodgings at Canterbury that afternoon.

Thomas Cranmer, Archbishop of Canterbury, had been appointed to lead the reception for Anne at Canterbury and he was also troubled by the weather, finding it difficult to get a sufficient number of people to come out to welcome the new queen. According to a letter from Cranmer to Cromwell, written on 29 December, the Archbishop had been forced to detain one of the minister's servants as:

> In case he and other gentlemen of the country, with mine own retinue, had not the better assisted me, over and besides the number appointed, I should have received her grace but with a slender company. For the whole number appointed to me, besides mine own company, was not six score, and yet some of them failed; so that if, partly by mine own company, and partly by other gentlemen's assistance, it had not been supplied, I should not have received her with a convenient number.

If Anne noticed the small number of people who received her at Canterbury, she was too polite to mention it. She was met on the downs outside Canterbury by the archbishop and four other bishops. Upon entering the town 'the mayor and citizens received her with torchlight and a good peal of guns' before she was brought to the former St Augustine's Abbey just outside the city walls. Upon arrival in her chamber Anne found '40 or 50 gentlewomen in velvet bonnets to see her, all which she took very joyously and was so glad to see the king's subjects resorting so lovingly to her, that she forgot all the foul weather and was very merry at supper'. Henry had converted the abbey into a comfortable palace for himself and it was a relief to Anne to get inside out of the rain. A feast was held in her honour that night, giving her the opportunity to become better acquainted with the archbishop and the other lords and ladies who had joined her train. Anne spent the night at Canterbury before travelling on to Sittingbourne on 30 December, staying one night before continuing her journey on New Year's Eve.

On the downs outside Rochester Anne was met by the Duke of Norfolk, Lord Dacre of the South, Lord Mountjoy and a large company of knights and esquires and the barons of the exchequer, all wearing velvet coats and gold chains. She was then conducted to the palace, where it was intended that she would spend New Year's Day. As she approached London, Anne's thoughts turned more and more to her first meeting with her future husband. Henry had been thinking of his future wife, too, and had followed Anne's progress closely since she had landed in England. Knowing that she would rest all day on New Year's Day, Henry, unable to contain his excitement any longer, decided to go in secret to see his bride for the first time, in order to 'norrishe love' between them.

The idea of a king visiting his new bride in secret was no innovation and Henry was following a centuries old tradition as he and five members of his Privy Chamber disguised in marble-coloured cloaks rode down from Greenwich to London to surprise Anne. In the chivalric tradition, the king was supposed to visit his bride in disguise and she, due to the love between them, was meant to immediately recognize her husband, in spite of the fact that the couple had never met. Henry already believed himself to be in love with Anne and he was certain that she would recognize him as her own love. It never crossed his mind that she would fail to recognize him and he ignored the example of his great-uncle, Henry VI, who had similarly visited his own bride, Margaret of Anjou, when she first landed in England. Henry VI's attempts to surprise his bride were a complete disaster. Henry VI took a letter to Margaret, disguised as a squire but she was so engrossed in reading the letter that she ignored him, keeping him on his knees. Once the king had gone one of Margaret's attendants asked her how she liked the squire but she replied: 'I did not notice him, as I was occupied in reading the letter he brought.' She was mortified when she learned the truth.

A number of accounts survive of the first meeting between Anne and Henry. The near contemporary Hall's Chronicle states that Henry, in disguise:

> Sodainly came to her presence, which therwill was sumwhat astonied: but after he had spoken and welcomed her, she with most gracious and loving countenaunce and behaviour him received and welcomed on her knees, whom he gently toke up and kissed: and all that after none commoned and devised with her, and that nyght supped with her, and the next day he departed to Grenewyche.

This was, perhaps, the official version of the meeting, intended to show the relationship between the king and the queen positively. It is clear from the accounts of those who were present that the meeting was very different indeed.

One of the men appointed to attend Henry was Sir Anthony Browne, a member of his privy chamber. Upon their arrival at Rochester, Henry ordered Browne to go to Anne to tell her that he had brought her a New Year's gift from the king. According to Browne:

> And when the said Sir Anthony entred the chambre where she was, and having conceived in his mind, what was by picture and advertisements signified of her beauty and qualities, at the general view of the ladies he thought he saw no such thing there, and yet were thither of better favour than the quene. But when he was directed unto herself, and advisedly loked upon her, he saith, he was never more dismayed in all his life, lamenting in his hart, which altered his outward countenance, to se the lady so far and

unlike that was reported, and of such sort as he thought the King's Highnes should not content himself with her. Nevertheles at his retorne to the Kings Majesty with her answer, the said Sir Anthony said nothing, ne durst not.

Anne was oblivious to Browne's reaction and, when Henry entered the room in disguise, she was standing at the window of her chamber watching bull-baiting in the courtyard below. Having met so many new people in the past few days, Anne did not look up when another stranger entered, intent on the spectacle below. Perhaps annoyed at the interruption, she paid the elderly and overweight stranger only the scantest of attention as he showed her a token that the king had sent.

Anne continued to watch the bull-baiting and Henry, seeing her disinterest in him, tried again, kissing and embracing her as she stood by the window. Anne was shocked at this attention; no other nobleman that she had met along the route had dared be so familiar with her. Unsure what to do Anne:

> Regarded him little, but always looked out of the window of the bull beating, and when the king perceaved she regarded his coming so little, he departed into [an]other chamber and putt of his cloke and came in againe in a cote of purple velvet; and when the lordes and knightes did see his Grace they did him reverence; and then she, perceiving the lordes doeing their dewties, humbled her Grace lowlie to the kinges Majestie, and his Grace saluted her againe, and so talked together lovinglie, and after tooke her by the hand and leed her into another chamber, where they solaced their graces that night and till Fridaie at afternoune; and then his Grace tooke his leave and departed thence to Gravesend, and theretooke his barge.

It was the worst possible start to their relationship. Anne's failure to recognize Henry shattered his romantic dreams and, in an instant, she was no longer his beloved. Anne should, perhaps, have realized that the only man in England who would dare to kiss and embrace the king's fiancée was the king himself but she was not expecting him and had not received an education in chivalric romance.

To add to the disaster, it was immediately noticed by Sir Anthony Browne and others who attended Henry that Anne was not quite what the king had been expecting and he 'noted in the kings Highnes countenance such a discontentment and misliking of her person, as he was very sory of it'. Henry's immediate dislike of Anne's appearance has been the subject of speculation for centuries. According to the eighteenth-century historian Smollett, Henry found Anne so different from her portrait that he swore that he had been brought a 'Flanders Mare' instead of a woman to wed. He is also alleged to have noted that Anne 'had unsavoury smells about her'. In the nineteenth century it was claimed that Anne had a large, loose and corpulent figure and that she was brown and swarthy. Several nineteenth-century historians also claimed that Anne had black hair but chose to wear a blond and highly unflattering wig for special occasions. While such comments are part of the legend that has built up around the first meeting rather than fact, it is evident that Henry took an instant dislike to Anne's appearance at Rochester.

Henry's reaction to Anne leads to speculation about her appearance. Surviving portraits of Anne are pleasant enough and she compares favourably to both Jane Seymour and Catherine Howard, supposedly the fairest of Henry's wives. Henry also never punished Holbein for his portrait of Anne, retaining his confidence in him as an artist until Holbein's death, suggesting that the portrait was a true likeness. One clue may lie in the fact that, unusually, Holbein painted Anne facing forwards. X-rays of a second portrait of Anne, painted with a side view, show that the portrait originally had a longer nose and Anne may have had a longer nose than would conventionally be called beautiful. A large nose can hardly be the only reason for Henry's rejection of Anne, and Nicholas Wotton and the other ambassadors who saw her, even if she was swathed in unflattering clothes, made no comment on this.

Another clue to Anne's appearance is found in a dispatch of Marillac, the French ambassador, on 5 January 1540. According to Marillac:

> The queen of England has arrived who, according to some who saw her close, is not so young as was expected, nor so beautiful as everyone affirmed.

She is tall and very assured in carriage and countenance, showing that in her turn and vivacity of wit supplies the place of beauty. She brings from her brother's country 12 or 15 damsels inferior in beauty even to their mistress and dressed so heavily and unbecomingly that they would be thought ugly even if they were beautiful.

Marillac further commented that Anne 'looks about 30 years of age, tall and thin, of medium beauty, and of very assured and resolute countenance'. While Marillac was critical of Anne's appearance, he did admit that she was the fairest of the ladies who had travelled with her from Cleves. Her heavy German clothes were seen as unflattering in England where the more simple French fashions were commonly worn and this contributed to the unfavourable opinion that Marillac formed of Anne's appearance. The worst that he said about her was that she looked older than she truly was. But Anne Boleyn was almost certainly over thirty when she married the king, as was Catherine Parr. Jane Seymour was twenty-seven or twenty-eight. Appearing to be around thirty years old should not, therefore, have been a bar to Henry finding Anne attractive. Lord Russell, one of Henry's attendants at Rochester, when pressed by Henry on Anne's attractiveness, also admitted that 'he toke her not for faire, but to be of a brown complexion'. However, Henry had known that Christina of Milan had dark skin and was still smitten with her portrait and determined to marry her. Jane Seymour had been unusually fair but Anne Boleyn, a woman who inspired passion in Henry, had been of dark colouring.

There is also evidence from those that had seen Anne that some people thought her pleasing enough. One contemporary who had perhaps seen Anne, reported to Cromwell in November 1539 that he 'gives praise to God for the alliance with the most illustrious, beautiful, and noble lady Anna de Cleves, who had a great gift from God, both of sense and wit. It would be difficult to describe her good manners and grace'. Of all the reports obtained from ambassadors during the negotiations, only the report of John Hutton back in December 1537 had been unfavourable where he stated to Cromwell that 'there is no great praise either of her personage or her beauty'. He wrote from Brussels where, in all likelihood, no one had ever seen Anne and the conclusion that must be drawn from the ambassadors' reports is that Anne was not by any means ugly. At the time of Henry's sixth marriage to Catherine Parr in 1543, Anne complained that Catherine was 'inferior to her in beauty'. This comment was not challenged and the Imperial Ambassador, Eustace Chapuys, agreed that Catherine was 'by no means so handsome as she [Anne] herself is'. Clearly, Anne, if tall and dark skinned, was by no means ill-favoured and many of her contemporaries found her attractive once she wore more flattering clothes. Henry VIII, unfortunately, did not.

It has been suggested by one historian that Henry's immediate unfavourable reaction to Anne may have been caused by the discovery, upon his arrival at Rochester, that her brother's ambassadors had not brought the proof that Anne's betrothal to Francis of Lorraine had truly been broken off. According to this theory, this caused Henry to immediately suspect that Anne was not, in fact, free to marry and that her brother was attempting to cover this up in order to push Henry into an alliance with her. This argument is possible but, given the fact that he had formed his negative opinion of Anne within minutes of his arrival at Rochester, it seems more likely that Henry's dislike was based purely on attraction. Henry had been married three times before and each time he had known his bride personally before the marriage and had formed an attraction to them. With Anne, on the other hand, Henry was forced to rely on portraits and descriptions and she simply did not appeal to him. What Henry failed to appreciate is that the shock was equally great on Anne's side.

Early in the marriage negotiations with Cleves, it had been proposed that William should marry Mary, Henry's eldest daughter. This was mentioned in Cromwell's instructions to Christopher Mont in January 1539 and the ambassador was instructed to refuse any request for a portrait of Mary as 'he ought to remember that her degre is suche, being the kinges doughter that of noo tyme it hath been seen, that the pictures of such shuld be sent abrodd'. Henry felt that it was beneath his daughter's dignity for her portrait to be sent to a potential suitor and, without doubt, Anne was not given the chance to inspect Henry's portrait before the marriage contract was signed. Women were rarely given the opportunity to see portraits of their own potential husbands and, while Charles V's sister Isabella of Austria was provided with a portrait of her own future husband, this was very unusual. Anne would instead have been forced to rely on snippets of information about Henry. She was certainly aware that he was older than her but she is unlikely to have been given a very up to date description of him. In his youth, Henry had been famous across Europe for his handsome face and athletic figure, with one contemporary describing him as 'the handsomest potentate I ever set eyes on; above the usual height, with an extremely fine calf to his leg, his complexion very fair and bright, with auburn hair combed straight and short, in the French fashion, and a round face so very beautiful, that it would become a pretty woman'. This description dates to 1515 but, if Anne had any idea of what her husband was like at all, it would have been based more on this out of date ideal than any recent description of Henry.

Anne cannot have imagined that Henry would have changed quite as much as he had from the handsome young king to the prematurely old, obese and decrepit man who stood before her. In January 1540, Henry was forty-eight years old and his handsome youth was far behind him. A more accurate portrayal of Henry was provided by Marillac later in the year when he described Henry as 'tainted' with the vices of covetousness, distrust, lightness and inconstancy and, by 1540, the king was a fearsome prospect. Anne also provided her own impression of Henry. According to the near-contemporary *Chronicle of Henry VIII*, at the time of his marriage to Catherine Parr, Anne exclaimed 'a fine burthen Madam Katharine has taken on herself!' in reference to the fact that Henry 'was so stout that such a man has never been seen. Three of the biggest men that could be found could get inside his doublet'. Henry and Anne were physically hopelessly incompatible but it was Anne who received the worst side of the bargain and her dismay at the realization of who the stranger was may have been as evident on her face as Henry's disappointment was on his.

According to Henry's own account of the meeting:

When the first communication was had with me for the marriage of the lady Anne of Cleves, I was glad to hearken to it, trusting to have some assured friend by it; I much doubting that time, both the emperor, and France, and the Bishop of Rome; and also because I heard so much, both of her excellent beauty and virtuous conditions. But when I saw her at Rochester, the first time that ever I saw her, it rejoiced my heart that I had kept me free from making any pact or bond before with her till I saw her myself; for then I assure you I liked her so ill, and so far contrary to that she was praised, that I was woe that ever she came into England.

Henry spent the night at Rochester waiting for the tide to change before hurrying away in the morning. His disappointment was such that he could not even bring himself to give Anne the rich furs and sables that he had brought as her New Year's present and he instead instructed Sir Anthony Browne to give them. In the boat on the way to Greenwich, Henry complained to Browne: 'I see nothing in this woman as men report of her; and I mervail that wise men would make such report as they have done.' He also questioned Lord Russell on his opinion of Anne, lamenting: 'Alas! Whom should men trust? I promise you, saith he, I se no such thing in her as hath been shewed me of her, and am ashamed, that men have so praysed her as they have don, and I like her not.'

It was for Cromwell, who had been so involved in the negotiations for the match, that Henry reserved the worst of his ire. Upon his arrival at Greenwich, the minister sought him out, asking him how he liked Anne. Henry answered heavily that she was 'nothing so well as she was spokyn of saying ferther that yf your highness hadde known as moche before as ye then knew she shold not haue commen within this Realme'. Henry demanded a remedy but there was nothing that Cromwell could do and he said 'I knew none but was veraye sory therffore and so god knoweth I was'. Henry wanted a solution, not sympathy, but matters were too far advanced to change course. Anne must also have spent a sleepless night as she considered the reality of her husband but she was just as powerless and, on 2 January, she made her way towards Dartford, the last stop on her journey before London.

6

A Great Yoke to Enter Into:
3 January – 5 January 1540

While Mistress Gilmyn had taught Anne some basic English by early 1540, Anne was still forced to communicate mainly by interpreters. This made conversation with Henry during the visit to Rochester difficult and it is likely that Anne did not realize the extent of the king's dislike of her. From her point of view she felt that she had hidden her own disappointment from him well and she knew there was no way out of the marriage. Anne was forced to press on and she kept her countenance cheerful as she prepared for her official welcome to England.

Henry had originally intended to meet Anne for the first time at her reception on Blackheath and he had prepared a grand event to welcome her. Most of the organization for the reception fell to Cromwell and he was determined that it should be magnificent, instructing the people of London to come out to meet Anne. To everyone's relief, the weather on 3 January was fair, though the ground must have been wet and muddy. According to *Hall's Chronicle*, near the foot of Shooter's Hill at Blackheath, a rich pavilion made of cloth of gold was pitched, along with several other tents. In each tent fires were set and the air perfumed in order to provide a place for Anne to rest and change her clothes. In a line from the tents to the gates of the park at Greenwich, the trees and bushes were also all cut down in order to show the assembled crowd at their best:

> About xii of the clocke her grace with al the company which were of her owne nacion to the number of a C [100] horse, and accompanied with the dukes of Norffolke and Suffolke, the Archebyshop of Caunterbury and other bysshops, lords and knightes whiche had received and conveyed her as you

have hard before, came doune shoters hyl toward the tentes, and a good space from the tentes met her the erle of Rutland her lorde Chamberleyn, sir Thomas Denyce her Chauncellor, and all her councellers and officers, amongst whom, doctor Daye appointed to her Almoner, made to her an eloquent oracion in latin, presenting to her on the kynges behalf all the officers and servauntes: whiche oracion was aunswered unto by the Duke her brothers Secretarie there being present, whiche done, the lady Margarete Doglas, daughter to the Quene of Scottes, the lady Marques Dorcet, daughter to the Frenche Quene being nieces to the kyng, and the Duches of Rychemond, and the Countesse of Rutland and Herfford with divers other ladies and gentlewomen, to the number of xv saluted and welcomed her grace, whiche alighted out of her chariot in the which she had ridden all her long journey, and with most goodly demeanour and loving countenaunce gave to them hertie thankes and kissed them al, and after all her counsellors and officers kissed her hand, which done, she with al the ladies entered the tentes and there warmed them a space.

For Anne, her arrival at Blackheath signified the end of her journey from Cleves and she was glad to finally leave her chariot behind. She rested in the tent for a time, talking to her ladies and becoming acquainted with them as well as she could through interpreters. When she heard that the king had arrived she left the tent wearing a rich dress of cloth of gold with a round skirt in the German style. On her head she wore a cowl and over that a round cap set with pearls. Her hair was covered by black velvet and, around her neck she wore rich stones. Anne's dress looked outlandish and foreign to the assembled English court but she looked every inch the queen as she mounted a horse trapped out in finery and rode to greet the king.

As soon as Henry heard that Anne had arrived at her pavilion, he set out with his own train of gentlemen from nearby Greenwich palace. Henry was mounted on a richly trapped horse and, in spite of his age and infirmities, he looked magnificent. According to Hall's Chronicle:

His persone was apparelled in a coate of purple velvet, somewhat made lyke a frocke, all over embroidered with flatte golde of Damaske with small lace mixed between of the same gold and other laces of the same so goyng traverse wyse, that the ground little appered: about whiche garment was a ryche garde very curiously embroidered, the sleves and brest were cut, lined with cloth of golde, and tied together with great buttons of Diamondes, Rubyes, and Orient Perle, his sworde and swordgyrdle adorned with stones and especial Emerodes, his night cappe garnished with stone, but his bonnet was so ryche of Juels that fewe men coulde value them. Besyde all this he ware in baudrike wyse a coller of such Balistes and Perle that few men ever sawe the lyke.

The couple came forward to meet each other on horseback, Henry disguising any distaste he felt for Anne and showing 'a moste lovely countenaunce and princely behaviour'. Anne and Henry then embraced and Anne, 'with most amiable aspect and womanly behaviour received his grace with many swete words and greate thankes and praisynges geven to hym'. Anne had rehearsed her speech in English and she was word perfect. The Chronicler, Hall, was quite overcome with the spectacle, commenting: 'O what a sight was this to se so goodly a prince and so noble a kyng to ryde with so fayre a lady of so goodly a stature and so womanly a countenaunce.' They then rode together through the lane of people to the sound of drums and trumpets and followed by their respective retinues.

Anne's reception at Greenwich was the grandest pageant on her long journey to England and she charmed the waiting crowds with her regal demeanour. Both she and Henry put on a show of loving harmony and, as they entered the courtyard to the palace, the couple dismounted. Henry then embraced Anne and kissed her, bidding her welcome before leading her through the hall. He took her personally to the queen's apartments where he left her to settle in. Henry had behaved with courtesy towards Anne throughout the reception and no one in the crowd noticed any difficulty between the royal couple. Anne was grateful for the attention and, in spite of her own disappointment at her husband, she had no idea that there was anything wrong in Henry's reaction to her.

In spite of Henry's courtesy towards his fiancée, the official reception of Anne had not changed his opinion of her. According to Thomas Cromwell:

The next daye after the recept of the said ladye and her enterye made in to grenwyche and after your highness hadde brought her to her chamber I then waytyd vppon your highness unto your privey chamber, and being ther your grace callyd me to yow saying to me this words or the lyke my lorde is it not as I told yow say what they will she is nothing so fayre as she hathe bene reportyd, howbeit she is well and semelye, whereunto I answered saying by my faythe syr ye saye trewthe, adding thereunto that yet I thought she hadde a quenlye manner, and neuertheles was sorye that your grace was no better content.

While Henry did praise Anne's manner, he was unable to find anything else about her that appealed to him and Cromwell was forced to admit that she was not the beauty that Henry had been promised.

Anne and Henry's marriage was scheduled for the day after the reception but Henry, desperate for the ceremony to be cancelled, instructed Cromwell to gather his council in the evening of 3 January to try to find a way out for the king. Broken betrothals were often used as a means of securing an annulment. Conveniently, Henry and his Council were aware of Anne's broken betrothal to Francis of Lorraine and this was immediately seized upon as a way out of the marriage for Henry. The council wasted no time in summoning Olisleger and Hochsteden, the two ambassadors of Anne's brother, and demanded to see documents proving that Anne's betrothal had been sufficiently broken off and that she was free to marry. The two ambassadors, baffled by the sudden request when everything seemed to be going so well, asked to be given until the next morning to make their answer.

It has recently been argued by one historian that a request to see evidence of Anne's eligibility to marry was entirely appropriate and that the ambassadors must have expected this. In this analysis, the ambassadors apparently dreaded the time that they would be expected to provide proof as they had none. It was also suggested that the fact that Anne may not have been free to marry was the real reason behind Henry's rejection of her. This argument does not stand up to close analysis however and, while it was indeed usual for a prospective groom to seek evidence that his bride was free to marry in circumstances such as Anne and Henry's, it was certainly not usual for the groom to wait until the eve of the wedding before making such a demand. The time to raise such concerns was during the negotiations for the marriage and, at the time that the marriage contract was signed, the English negotiators were apparently perfectly happy with the assurance that the betrothal had never been binding on Anne and Francis as minors and that it had been declared void publicly in Cleves. Henry's real reason for desiring proof that Anne was free to wed in the days before the marriage is also clear from the report of his brother-in-law and friend, the Duke of Suffolk. Suffolk, noting Henry's unhappiness with Anne, commented that Henry 'would have been glad, if the solemnization might than to the world have been disappointed, without note of breach of his Highnes behalf'. Henry hoped desperately that no evidence would be produced.

Olisleger and Hochsteden were not expecting to be interrogated by the council only hours after Anne's triumphant reception. According to Cromwell:

> In the mornyng your sayd cownsaylors and they [the ambassadors] met erlye and ther eftsoons was purposyd vnto them aswell touching the comyssyon for the performaunce of the tretye and articles sent to Maister Wotton as also touching the contractes and covenauntes of mariage between the Duke of Lorayns son, and the Ladye Anne and what termes they stodde in, to the whiche thinges so purposyd thay answeryd as men moche perplexyd that as touching the commyssyon thay hadde none to trete consernyng the articles sent to Mr Wotton and as to the contractes and covenauntes of marriage they wolde say nothing but that a reuocacyon was made, and that thay were but spowsaylles.

Anne's betrothal to Francis of Lorraine had been abandoned so long ago that the necessary documents had been lost or no longer existed and, certainly, the ambassadors did not have them to hand. They were shocked at the sudden change in the council's attitude towards them and finally, in exasperation, the two ambassadors swore to remain as hostages in England until the necessary documents could be brought from Cleves.

By vouching that the documents existed, the two ambassadors closed the door to Henry's escape route and Cromwell rushed to speak to the king, using the back stairs of the palace to avoid being seen. According to Cromwell, Henry was furious at the outcome of his council's efforts, roaring to Cromwell that 'I am not well handelyd'. Henry had already convinced himself that some way out would be found and that he would not have to go through with the marriage and he continued saying to his minister that:

> yf it were not that she is com so farre into my realme and the great preparacyons that my states & people hathe made for her and for fere of making of a ruffull in the woorlde that is the meane to dryve her brother into the hands of the emperowre and Frenche kynges hands being now to gether I woolde neuer have ne marye her.

Henry was right to be fearful that any rejection of Anne would drive William into an alliance with the emperor or the King of France and the political situation in Europe had never looked more dangerous to Henry than it did in January 1540. Towards the end of 1539 Charles V had announced that he intended to travel from Spain to Flanders. Usually he would have made a long sea voyage but, this time, Francis I invited him to travel through France. Charles readily accepted and he travelled through the major cities of France as an honoured guest, reaching Paris at around the time of Anne's arrival in England. For Henry, the visit was ominous and, with the news of the ambassadors' assurances that the betrothal had been broken, Henry had only one further straw at which to clutch.

Henry considered what to do over dinner that day and, following his meal, he once again summoned his council. The council deliberated for some time and finally both the Archbishop of Canterbury and the Bishop of Durham suggested that, in the event that Anne and Francis had been betrothed, a renunciation from either party was necessary to break the engagement legally. This was Henry's last hope and he stalked out of the council chamber ordering his ministers to ask Anne to give a verbal renunciation of any betrothal before notaries. Henry cannot have had high hopes that Anne would refuse and he was right. Anne was perplexed to be summoned to swear that she was free from any precontract, but she did so willingly, perhaps assuming it to be an English custom. Trembling, Cromwell took the news to Henry who answered furiously: 'Is there none other remedye but that I must nedes agenst my will put my neck in the yoke.' Cromwell , usually so assured in finding solutions to any problem that faced the king, had nothing to say and left Henry alone.

Once Henry had accepted the inevitable, he allowed preparations for the marriage to continue and he attended mass that day with Anne, making no show of his disappointment. On the following day he signed three documents granting Anne lands as part of her dower. The total value of lands listed was nearly 700 marks and Anne was generously provided for, something that must have been satisfying both for her and for the unsettled ambassadors. Anne's household had been appointed in preparation for her arrival and she was given time to get to know her officers and ladies while she waited for her wedding. An appointment in the queen's household was a coveted one and Anne's household was headed by the Earl of Rutland as her chamberlain. Other gentlemen were appointed as her chancellor, master of horse, secretary and receiver general and she was also provided with her own surveyor, auditor, attorney and solicitor. Anne had a cupbearer, ushers, servers and her own sergeant at arms, as well as clerks and a chaplain. Anne greeted the men and enquired into their roles during the days following her arrival at Greenwich.

Anne's ladies were intended to be her companions at court. Chief among the ladies were those that had welcomed her at the reception to Greenwich and included the king's niece, Lady Margaret Douglas, and his daughter-in-law, the Duchess of Richmond, the widow of his illegitimate son. Anne was also to be attended by the Duchess of Suffolk who was, by that time, a familiar face to her, as well as the Countess of Suffolk and Lady Rochford, the sister-in-law of Anne Boleyn. In a move that Anne no doubt approved of, Mistress Gilmyn was appointed to wait upon her, as was Anne Bassett, the daughter of Lady Lisle. Anne appeared as obliging to these ladies as she had done in Calais to Lady Lisle and they were relieved to find their mistress so kindly.

In the evening of 5 January, two days later than originally planned, Anne was informed that her marriage was to take place the next day. In spite of her disappointment over her husband, Anne, since arriving in England, had never had any doubts that she would marry the king and indeed would have brought shame on her family if she had even attempted to refuse Henry. She made her preparations for the wedding with her ladies, anxious at just what marriage to Henry would be like. Henry was also anxious that evening and, when Sir Anthony Browne came to him 'he saw the king's highness nothing pleasantly disposed, but heard him say, that he had a great yoke to enter into'. The language barrier and Henry's ability to appear warm and affectionate to Anne in public meant that she had no idea that, the night before her wedding, the king was as pensive about the marriage as she.

7

To Satisfy the World:
6 January 1540 – February 1540

Both Anne and Henry woke with trepidation on the morning of 6 January 1540. Both awoke early and set about separately making their preparations for the wedding ceremony with heavy hearts.

Anne rose early and, with the help of her ladies, prepared herself for her wedding. She had brought a magnificent trousseau of clothes and jewels with her to England. She had saved her richest dress for the marriage ceremony and her appearance made an impression with the chronicler, Edward Hall, recording that she wore:

> A gowne of ryche cloth of gold set full of large flowers of great and orient pearle, made after the Dutche fassion rownde, her here [hair] hangyng downe, whiche was faire, yellow and long. On her head a coronal of gold replenished with great stone, and set about full of braunches of rosemary, about her necke and middle, juelles of great valew and estimacion.

Anne had grown up wearing the heavier fashions and round skirts popular in Germany and the Low Countries and she had no idea that, while the richness of her dress was commented upon, it was also generally felt that it did nothing for her appearance.

Henry was dressed equally richly and, with his height and girth, was an over-awing sight in his 'gowne of clothe of gold, raised with flowers of sylver, furred with blacke jenettes, his cote crimosyn sattyn all to cutte and embroidered and tied with great diamonds, and a ryche coller about his necke'. In spite of the richness of his clothing, it was clear to everyone that Henry's heart was not in the marriage and his friend, Sir Anthony Browne, later commented that Henry 'prepared himself so slakely to go to the chapel to make solemnisation, as in his countenance, fashion, and behaviour he declared evidently, that he went to do that act, as hym thought, wheunto his Grace was not moved, ne directed by his entire and harty consent'. Henry made it quite clear to everyone that he went to marry Anne under duress and he commented to Cromwell as he made his way to the chapel that he did what he must needs do. Of Henry's six marriages, it was certainly his most sombre.

The Earl of Essex had been appointed to lead Anne to the church and she waited patiently for his arrival with her ladies. Even this did not go smoothly and, when Essex failed to arrive on time, Henry dismissively sent Cromwell to Anne to lead her to church instead. Cromwell was anxious at the way the king associated him with his hated fiancée but he was determined to please and went scurrying to Anne, finding her ready in her chamber. As Cromwell arrived, Essex also appeared and the minister hurried back to the king in time to make his way to the chapel with Henry. As Cromwell reached Henry the king commented: 'My lorde yf it were not to satisfye the world and my Realme I woolde not doo that I must doo this day for none erthlye thing.' Henry then stalked out of the room towards the chapel.

Henry reached the gallery outside the chapel at around eight o'clock in the morning and paused to wait for Anne. Anne had set out at about the same time, escorted by the Earls of Essex and Overstein. According to *Hall's Chronicle*, Anne with 'moste demure countinaunce and sad behaviour, passed thorough the kynges chamber, all the lords goyng befor her till they came to the gallery where the kyng was, to whom she made thre low obeysaunces and curtesies'. Anne and Henry then moved into the chapel and Archbishop Cranmer performed the ceremony with Overstein taking the role of Anne's brother and giving her away. Anne performed what must have been a daunting task perfectly and she spoke quietly during the marriage service before receiving a ring from Henry engraved with the words 'God send me wel to kepe'. Neither Anne nor Henry showed any discomfiture to the other and, once they were married, they walked hand in hand to the king's closet where they heard mass together. The couple then parted, going to their separate chambers to prepare for the rest of the day.

With her marriage, Anne was finally Queen of England and she found herself attended as such. According to Hall's Chronicle, Anne and Henry rested for a short time and then shortly after 9 o'clock in the morning Henry came to Anne's chamber and led her to mass with him. The couple then dined together before Anne changed her clothes, dressing in 'a gowne lyke a mannes gowne, of tissue with longe sleves gyrte to her, furred with ryche sables, her narowe sleves were very costly, but on her head she had a cap as she ware on the saterdaie before with a cornet of laune, whiche cap was so ryche of perle and stone, that it was judged to bee of greate valew'. Her ladies were dressed in a similar fashion and she led them into the chapel for Evensong, accompanied by the king. Anne and Henry supped together that evening before enjoying 'bankettes, maskes, and diverse dysportes, tyll the tyme came that it pleased the kyng and her to take their rest'.

Anne behaved like a queen throughout the afternoon and evening of her wedding day, talking pleasantly to Henry through their interpreters. Henry was also kind and solicitous to Anne and never let her know his private feelings towards her and, as the day went on, some of Anne's dreads about the marriage passed. For all his fearsome reputation and unappealing appearance, Anne may well have thought that she could do worse in a husband. Henry also attempted to make the best of the marriage and, at the end of the celebrations, the couple retired to bed together in order to consummate their marriage.

Anne and Henry were ceremonially put to bed by the members of their court before being left alone together for the first time. Henry had been married three times before, as well as having had several mistresses, and was well versed in what was required of him as a husband. There is, however, some dispute over precisely what Anne was expecting when she prepared herself to spend the night with her husband. In June 1540 three of Anne's ladies, Ladies Rutland, Rochford and Edgecombe, reported a conversation that they had apparently had with Anne around midsummer at Westminster Palace. According to the report of the ladies:

First, al they being together, they wished her Grace with child. And she answered and said, she knew wel she was not with child. My lady Edgecombe said, how is it possible for your Grace to know that, and ly every night with the king? I know it wel I am not, said she. Than said my lady Edgecombe, I think your Grace is a mayd stil. With that she laughed. And than said my lady Rocheford, by our lady, Madam, I think your Grace is a mayd stil, indeed. How can I be a mayd, said she, and slepe every night with the king? There must be more than that, said my lady Rocheford, or els I had as leve the king lay further. Why, said she, when he comes to bed he kisses me, and taketh me by the hand, and byddeth me, Good night, swete hart: and in the morning kisses me, and byddeth me, Farewel, darling. Is not thys enough? Then said my lady Rutland, Madam there must be more than this, or it wil be long or we have a Duke of York, which al this realm most desireth. Nay, said the Quene, is not this enough? I am contented with this, for I know no more. Then said my lady Rutland, did not your Grace tel Mother Low this? Then said the Quene, mary, fy-fy, for shame. God forbid.

This conversation is generally taken to have been evidence that Anne was entirely ignorant of just what was expected of her as Henry's wife. In the sixteenth century it was commonly considered to be the bride's mother's duty to provide her daughter with a good knowledge of sexual intercourse and it is inconceivable that Maria of Juliers would have left her daughter so ill-prepared for what she would face as a wife. The reported conversation between Anne and her ladies must also be considered suspect and, in order for Anne to speak in such detail to her ladies by midsummer 1540, it implies knowledge of the English language that she simply could not have possessed. As late as June 1540 Anne's lord chancellor, the Earl of Rutland, complained that he needed an interpreter to be able to understand her and it is impossible that she could have had such an intimate conversation in a language that she had, at most, only started learning six months before. If the conversation occurred at all, it must have been full of misunderstandings and confusion on both sides and it is not impossible that the ladies would have falsified Anne's reported comments as a way of pleasing the king when he was seeking a divorce.

On balance, it seems likely that Anne was indeed aware of just what was expected of her on her marriage night. As Henry later himself reported the marriage night did not go quite as either he or Anne had imagined and 'I never for love to the woman consented to marry; nor yet if she brought maidenhead with her, took any from her by true carnal copulation'. The following morning Henry also gave Cromwell a full account of exactly what had happened which the minister faithfully reported some months later. According to Cromwell he found the king in his privy chamber and asked Henry how he liked the queen. Henry replied: 'Surlye my lorde as ye know I lykyd her befor not well but now I lyke her moche worse for quoth your highnes I have felte her belye and her brestes and therby as I can judge she sholde be noe mayde which strake me so to the harte when I felt them that I hadde nother will nor corage to procede any ferther in other matyers.' After running his hands over Anne's body Henry came to the conclusion that she could not be a virgin, blaming this for his disinclination to consummate the marriage that night. Henry further clarified his comments, telling Sir Thomas Hennege that Anne could not possibly be a virgin due to the 'loseness of her brests, and other tokens'. He also complained that she smelled. It appears that Anne's body was more what Henry expected of a married woman who had borne children. Given Anne's cosseted upbringing with her mother, it is impossible that she had ever had a lover and she was certainly a virgin on her wedding night. As Henry's later debacle with Catherine Howard would show he was certainly no expert in determining whether or not a woman was a virgin.

Henry complained that he doubted Anne's virginity, but he also admitted to Sir Thomas Hennege that he had been unable to physically consummate the marriage, finding himself unable to 'do as a man should do with his wife'. Henry made the same comments to Anthony Denny, a gentleman of his privy chamber, stating that 'he could never in her company be provoked and stered to know her carnally'. Henry had become intermittently impotent during his marriage to Anne Boleyn and the subject of his impotency was raised at the trial of Anne's brother, Lord Rochford. At the time of his marriage to Jane Seymour, there were also comments that the king might have difficulty in consummating the marriage and the king himself was doubtful that he would be able to father a child with his third wife. With Jane's pregnancy and the subsequent birth of Prince Edward, Henry's impotency was forgotten but it reappeared worryingly for both Henry and Anne of Cleves on their wedding night.

While Henry blamed Anne for his failure to consummate their marriage, he was sufficiently worried to consult his physicians, Dr Chamber and Dr Butts, on the morning after the wedding. The doctors warned Henry 'not to enforce himself, for eschewing such inconveniences as by debility ensueing in that case were to be feared'. Henry took this advice seriously, spending the second night after the wedding alone. On the third night, he and Anne made another attempt to consummate the marriage but, again, Henry was forced to confess to his doctors that 'he could not know her'. Henry continued in his attempts most nights, still regularly consulting with his doctors and he informed them secretly how he 'found her body in such a sort disordered and indisposed to excite and provoke any lust in hym; yea, rather ministering mattier of loathsomeness unto the same'. Henry also made it plain to the doctors that the problem was Anne's and not his, confessing to a number of 'wet dreams' during the nights that he was unable to perform with her.

Impotency was an embarrassing condition for a man in Tudor England and one which most men would not willingly admit to. In the early seventeenth century a famous divorce case was brought by Lady Frances Howard against her husband, the Earl of Essex on the grounds of his impotency and the record of these proceedings shows the embarrassment that was felt by the Earl. When questioned on the subject by the then Archbishop of Canterbury, the Earl avowed 'the ability of himself for generation; and that he was resolv'd never to lay any blemish upon himself that way'. With the Earl's refusal to confirm his wife's claims, it was recognized that it would be very difficult to proceed with the suit. According to the Archbishop, it was necessary to proceed upon either confession or proof and 'that as was probable, the Earl would not confess his Own Impotency, for then he blemish'd himself'. Most men would never admit to impotency under any circumstances and the fact that rumours quickly circulated about the state of Henry and Anne's marriage must have been deeply worrying for the queen.

During the early weeks of their marriage, Henry continued to spend at least every second night with Anne in the hope that he would be able to consummate the marriage. While he had made his revulsion of her quite clear, the political situation in Europe meant that both Anne and Henry were forced to attempt to make the most of their marriage. Further evidence that Anne was fully aware that there was a problem can be found in her desperate attempts during the months of her marriage to speak to Cromwell alone. Anne recognized that Cromwell was one of the ministers closest to the king and she was anxious to try to make her marriage work regardless of her own disappointment in Henry. Cromwell, who was already concerned about his perceived association with Anne, did not dare to speak to her and instead reported her attempts to speak with him to the king. Henry gave the minister permission to speak directly to Anne, commenting that Cromwell 'myght do moche good in ofering to her to be playn with her in declaring my mynde'. It would have been a delicate conversation and Cromwell had no stomach for it, instead seeking out Anne's Lord Chamberlain, the Earl of Rutland, and asking him 'to fynde som mean that the queen might be induced to order your grace pleasantlye in her behaveour towards yow [Henry]'. Cromwell also later called Rutland and the rest of Anne's council to him and 'requeryd them to cownsayle thayr mastres to vse all pleasauntries to your Highnes'. It is unclear whether any of these men did pluck up the courage to speak to Anne. She was already, in any event, aware that there was a problem and did her best to try to attract the king.

According to *Hall's Chronicle*, a joust was held at Greenwich in celebration of Anne's marriage. Perhaps already noting the comments about her German dress, Anne tried to please Henry by dressing in the English fashion as the ladies of his court did. She also wore a French hood, the daring head covering made popular in England by Anne Boleyn which showed her hair in front of the jewelled band. Henry was known to favour this manner of dress and the chronicler commented that the hood and dress 'so set furthe her beautie and good visage, that every creature rejoysed to behold her'. Henry however did not and, with the continued failure of her marriage, Anne finally gave up her attempts to please him. To add insult to injury, Anne and Henry do not seem to have got on well outside the bedchamber either and, after only a few weeks of marriage, Henry complained to Cromwell that he 'hadde sume communicacyon with her of my ladye Marye how that she began to wax stoborne and wylfull'. The details of Anne and Henry's argument are not clear but it may have been Anne attempting to assert some authority in a marriage that was rapidly moving out of her control. There was no one that Anne could safely talk to about the difficulties in her marriage in England and she was too embarrassed to admit there was a problem to her family in Cleves, instead sending a message to her mother and brother 'that she thanked them most heartily for having preferred her to such a marriage that she could wish no better'. Anne and Henry also wrote to Anne's brother and mother in late January giving no indication of the problems in their relationship.

In spite of their personal difficulties, Anne remained Henry's queen and, publicly at least, he was committed to the marriage. Anne spent the first few weeks of her marriage at Greenwich then, on 4 February, she moved with the court to Westminster. Henry gave her a grand pageant as the court journeyed by water, as befitted the first entry of his queen to London. According to *Wriothesley's Chronicle*:

First, his Graces [household] going in barges afore his Majesty, then his Grace going in his barge and his gard following in another barge; then the Quene in her barg and her ladies followinge in another barge, and then her household servants, then the Mayor and Aldermen of London in a barge and tenne of the cheiffe craftes of the cities following the mayor in their barges, which were all rychlie hanged with schuchions and targattes and banners of the cognisans of everie occupation, the Mercers barge hanged rychlie with cloath of gold; and from Greenewych to the Towre all the shipps which laie in the Thames shott gonnes as the kinge and queene passed by them. And when they came against the Tower their was shott within the Tower above a thousand chambers of ordinance which made a noyse like thunder; and that donne they passed through London Bridge to Westminster, the mayor and all the craftes following till they see their Grace on land, which was the first coming of the Queenes Grace to Westminster synce her Graces coming into Englande.

For all the grandeur of the occasion, it is telling that Anne and Henry did not travel in the same barge. In fact, by the time the court left Greenwich, the marriage had irretrievably broken down. Anne was well aware of this and, after weeks of humiliation in Henry's bed, gave up all hope of a personal relationship with him, instead concentrating on the public role of queen.

8

Queen Anne of Cleves:
February 1540 – May 1540

In spite of the immediate failure of her marriage, Anne was not prepared
to admit defeat and set out to prove herself as Queen of England.

Before Anne's arrival Henry had ordered her apartments at Greenwich
to be sumptuously fitted out. During November and December 1539 the
king's carpenters had been busy fitting a roof to the queen's new privy
kitchen and a new doorway linking this building to the king's. A new
door was also installed in the king's bedchamber, perhaps linking it more
directly with the queen's. Even after Henry and Anne were married, work
was carried out in the queen's apartments and the king's privy chamber. In
spite of this, preparations for Anne's coronation was abruptly forgotten
and, while originally planned for Whitsun, all mention of the ceremony
was quickly dropped, to Anne's disappointment.

As queen, Anne was expected to maintain a large household as a mark
of her rank. As soon as her marriage was announced, members of Henry's
court began to jostle for positions. In November 1539, for example, John
Gostwyk wrote to Cromwell asking him to 'remember young Catlyn, your
servant, to be in the queen's wardrobe'. At the same time, Jane Rooper
wrote to the chief minister to ask him to promote her son-in-law to be
attorney to the queen. While Anne was staying in Calais, Lord Lisle,
Henry's governor of the town, approached Dr Olisleger regarding an
appointment for his stepdaughter, Katharine Basset. It was soon apparent
to everyone that it was the king, not the queen, who had the final say, as
Olisleger reported to Lord Lisle on 6 January:

My lord, very sorry at heart I am to advertise you that with the knowledge and goodwill of the queen's grace I have spoken with the king our master and also with my Lord Privy Seal [Cromwell] and the other gentlemen of the Council, to have Mistress Katharine, your wife's daughter, to be of the Privy Chamber with the queen; to the which I have had answer made me that the ladies and gentlewomen of the Privy Chamber were appointed before her Grace's coming, and that for this time patience must be had. And however much I have earnestly prayed that the gentlewoman might be taken to be of the number of the others as only for the queen's pleasure, nevertheless I have received the same reply, for the which I am very sorry, and that I cannot at this time advertise you that I have done you pleasure in this your desire.

Anne was fond of Lady Lisle, who had entertained her so attentively in Calais, and she was anxious to do what she could to promote her daughter. Lady Lisle had spent much of Jane Seymour's time as queen pursuing an appointment for her daughters, Anne and Katharine, and had finally secured an appointment for Anne Basset, only for the queen to die within weeks. Anne Basset received an appointment in Anne's new household but Lady Lisle was once again forced to pursue a place for Katharine.

Lady Lisle was not prepared to give up on a position for Katharine and by February was sending wine and barrels of herring as gifts to Lady Rutland, one of Anne's chief ladies in the hope that she would petition Anne for a place for Katharine. Lady Rutland wrote thanking Lady Lisle but, once again, was forced to admit that the final decision lay with the king who had determined 'that no more maids shall be taken in'. She was however able to offer the hope that, if Lady Lisle were to approach Mother Lowe, a formidable lady whom Anne had brought with her from Cleves to be governor to the maids, she could 'do as much good in this matter as any one woman here, that she may make some means to get your said daughter with the queen's said grace; and in so doing, I think ye shall obtain your purpose in every behalf'. Lady Rutland promised to do all she could and she spoke directly to Katharine who wrote to her mother asking her to send some token to Mother Lowe so that she might the better remember her for a place.

A letter from Anne Basset to her mother setting out her own approach suggests the king's reasons behind his rejection of Katharine:

> And whereas you do write to me that I should remember my sister, I have spoken to the king's Highness for her, and his grace made me answer that Master Bryan and divers others hath spoken to his Grace for her friends, but he said he would not grant me nor them as yet; for his Grace said that he would have them that should be fair, and as he thought meet for the room.

Disappointed in Anne's appearance, Henry was determined to ensure that her household was filled with young ladies attractive to him and Katharine Basset was simply not attractive enough. Anne of Cleves also knew well enough that she had no influence over her husband and she was unable to insist on any appointments for her own household.

In spite of Katharine Basset's failure to meet Henry's stringent requirements regarding the beauty of Anne's maids, a niece of the Duke of Norfolk, Catherine Howard, had been with Anne's household from her arrival at Greenwich and she quickly caught the king's eye. Catherine Howard was several years younger that Anne and was born at some point between 1521 and 1525. By 1540 she was an orphan and had little to recommend her except her Howard blood and her uncle secured the appointment for her as a means of providing for one of his many penniless relatives. Norfolk hoped that Catherine, who was described by the French ambassador, Marillac, as 'a lady of great beauty' would find herself an eligible husband at court although it is not impossible that he would also have hoped that she might catch the king's eye as a potential mistress. Another of his nieces, Anne Boleyn, had, of course, risen to be Henry's second wife and while it is unlikely that, in late 1539, before Anne had even arrived, Norfolk was hoping that Catherine would replace her as queen, he would have welcomed the rise in his family's fortunes that a niece as the king's mistress would bring. At a second glance, Marillac decided that Catherine was not as beautiful as he had previously thought, commenting that she was more graceful than beautiful and extremely short. The king found her enchanting however, as was quickly noted at court.

Anne watched Catherine warily as Henry's interest become evident. Henry was famous for his rejection of his first wife, Catherine of Aragon, for her maid, Anne Boleyn, and Anne was anxious to ensure that the same did not happen to her. Once Henry's interest in Catherine and his lack of interest in the queen had been noticed, Norfolk and others of her party began to coach her in how to behave towards the king and she, like Anne Boleyn and Jane Seymour before her, determined not to surrender herself to the king without a promise of marriage. This was out of the question early in 1540, much to Anne's relief, but Henry continued to behave as though he was in love with Catherine. According to one report:

> This was first whispered by the courtiers, who observed the king to be much taken with another young lady of very diminutive stature, whom he now has. It is a certain fact, that about the same time many citizens of London saw the king very frequently in the day-time, and sometimes at midnight, pass over to her on the river Thames in a little boat. The Bishop of Winchester also very often provided feastings and entertainments for them in his palace; but the citizens regarded all this not as a sign of divorcing the queen, but of adultery.

Anne, hampered by her limited English, fervently hoped that this was the case. The fact that Stephen Gardiner, the conservative Bishop of Winchester, was actively involved in the promotion of Catherine Howard seemed ominous to Anne's friends.

Anne's household was headed by Ladies Rutland, Browne and Edgecombe as well as a number of ladies who had previously held appointments with Queen Jane. While Anne had always known that she would be expected to become an English queen, the loss of much of her German household was difficult for her. Within days of her marriage, much of her household were already planning to return home. Henry put on a public show of his contentment with the marriage, providing fine gifts to Anne's escort, including gilt cups of various values to the ambassadors and also to Lady Keteler, the chief of Anne's German ladies. Even Olisleger, who had been such a help to Anne both as translator and for the information he provided on English customs, was gone by the end of January and for Anne it must have seemed like a final break with home to see them go. It was a relief for Anne that some of her escort were permitted to remain with her in England, including Mother Lowe, upon whom she relied so heavily, and her young cousin, Count von Waldeck, all of whom were appointed to remain with her 'till she wer better acquainted in the realme'. Other members of Anne's train also received appointments in either the king's service or Cromwell's, providing further links to her homeland for Anne.

The return of Anne's escorts to Cleves and Saxony provided news of the marriage to Anne's family and congratulations began to pour in from Germany. John Frederick wrote to Henry following news of the marriage to express his congratulations, writing that 'our Counsellors, when they returned, shewed us that the beginning of the marriage of your royal Majesty was joyful and prosperous, which we desire God to bless and fortunately to continue'. Both Henry and Cromwell were determined that no word of his disappointment in Anne should reach Germany and Cromwell wrote to Henry's ambassadors on the Continent assuring them of Henry's happiness with the queen. Nicholas Wotton was also despatched once again to Cleves at the end of January, arriving on 9 February 1540 when he reported Henry and Anne's contentment with the marriage.

Anne's brother was glad of the news that the marriage was going so well and, by early 1540, it was becoming clear to everyone that he and the emperor were implacably opposed over the issue of Guelders. While Henry had first entered into an alliance with William because both were enemies of the emperor, it had always been assumed by the English that it would be Cleves coming to their aid in the event that they were attacked and not the other way around.

On 8 April, William sent for Wotton to inform him that the emperor's brother, Ferdinand, King of the Romans, had offered to mediate in the dispute over Guelders and that he intended to travel secretly to meet with Charles V to try to reach some agreement. Wotton informed William that he thought this a very strange course of action, and warned him of the dangers of putting his trust in his enemy, advising him instead to seek counsel from both Henry and John Frederick. He further stated that if William went without consulting Henry, the English king would 'maintain his friendship, but yet that he must suspect something in the matter'. Olisleger agreed with Wotton's point of view and informed him privately that William's counsel had warned him not to go 'but it was the Duke's own mind'. William promised to write to Henry and John Frederick, as well as Anne and Sibylla, to explain his reasoning, but he was determined to go ahead.

Wotton was asked by William to accompany him to meet the emperor at Ghent, as a gesture of his good faith. Wotton himself was convinced of William's friendliness towards England, something that was reassuring for Anne whose future lay in her new country. He was also particularly anxious to avoid war because, while Guelders was well fortified, it was well known that Juliers was unlikely to withstand any attack. William was therefore eager to reach agreement with the emperor but only providing that he continued to rule Guelders. According to Wotton's own report of the meeting:

> The Duke of Cleves has delivered to the king of the Romans a declaration of his right to Gueldres, of which Wyatt had a copy at his departure. The Emperor only made answer thereto on Sunday, and the King of the Romans caused the Emperor's answer, written in Dutch, to be read before the Duke and his Council, but would not give a copy, saying the case was so clear, he had better follow the Emperor's mind and deliver Guelders to him. The Duke said he could make very good answer, but if the Emperor must needs have Guelders it was needless to reason further, and seeing that he could do no more without the consent of the Duchess, his mother, to whom he had not spoken when he left the country.

This was recognized as the delaying tactic it was and the King of the Romans continued to press William, demonstrating that he was not the impartial mediator he had promised to be. For William, the emperor's intransigence was a personal slight and he later told Wotton that:

> he marvelled that the Emperor was so stiff when he was content that the last duke of Gueldres, who was continually his enemy, and had done him more

hurt than any other prince; and had no right in the world to Gueldres and never kept promise with the emperor, should have Gueldres for him and his posterity if God sent him any.

With matters at an impasse, William returned home secretly. For Anne, everything seemed impossibly distant and dangerous and it was with relief that she heard that William had returned home safely, in spite of Charles's increased enmity towards him.

For both Henry and Cromwell the fact that Charles V had begun to turn his attention towards William was ominous and Henry had no desire to involve himself in the Duke of Cleves's war. Throughout the dangerous early months of 1540, while there was still a danger of attack from either Charles or Francis, Henry continued to publicly show his support for his marriage, speaking of his desire to have children by Anne in the instructions that he sent to his Scottish ambassador in January, for example. Anne was recognized as Henry's queen internationally and Francis's sister, the Queen of Navarre, requested a portrait of Anne alongside pictures of Henry and his children in April. Apart from a visit to his children at Richmond in March, Henry remained with Anne throughout the first months of their marriage and the couple celebrated Easter together at Hampton Court. The weather that winter was particularly damp and foul but Anne always appeared dignified when she appeared with the king in public. She also dined privately with Henry in her chamber on 18 April following Henry's appointment of Cromwell as Earl of Essex, and the pair apparently conversed together pleasantly enough.

Anne appeared publicly as queen alongside Henry at the great jousts held to celebrate May Day at Westminster Palace. According to *Wriothesley's Chronicle*, the tournament was a great spectacle and it may originally have been planned as Anne's coronation tournament. The leading young men of Henry's court jousted over three days, all dressed in white velvet in the Burgundian style. Following the tournament on 1 May:

The said chalengers rode to Durham Place, where they kept open howseholde, which said place was richlie behanged, and great cubbordes of plate, where they feated the kinges majestie, the queens Grace and her ladies, with all the court, and for all other comers that would resort to their said place, where they had all delicious meates and drinckes so plenteouslie as might be, and such melody of minstrelsy, and were served everie meale with their owne servants after the manner of war.

For Anne, who had had such a closeted upbringing in Cleves, the spectacle was magnificent. The public role of queen was something that she both enjoyed and excelled at and no one, except the king himself, had a bad word to say about her.

Anne rapidly became popular in England, particularly with the followers of the religious reform many of whom, mistaking her religious beliefs, hoped that she would bring Protestantism with her. According to one reformer, John Butler, writing to the leading continental reformer, Henry Bullinger: 'The state and condition of that kingdom is much more sound and healthy since the marriage of the queen, than it was before. She is an excellent woman, and one who follows God: great hopes are entertained of a very extensive propagation of the gospel by her influence. There is now no persecution.' Anne retained her Catholic beliefs until her death and, while she never showed any allegiance to the pope, she was very far from being a Lutheran. She was therefore surprised to find herself as the figurehead of the reformist party in England. By Easter 1540, England had become a dangerous place for those who looked upon Anne as their figurehead and also for Thomas Cromwell, the architect of her marriage and of her position in England.

9
A Special Counsellor of the Match:
May – July 1540

Although in public all was well with Anne and Henry's marriage, in private Henry's displeasure was clear to the entire court. For Henry, his marriage to Anne was a great mistake and somebody would have to pay the price for that error.

Thomas Cromwell, the king's chief minister, is generally considered to have been the architect of Anne's marriage, with the seventeenth-century historian, Edward Herbert, describing him as 'a special counsellor of the match'. Cromwell had risen from very humble origins to become the king's leading advisor by around 1535. According to the Imperial ambassador, Eustace Chapuys, the minister was the son of a humble blacksmith. In his youth, Cromwell had been imprisoned for some offence and was forced to leave the country, travelling in Flanders, Italy and Rome. Upon his return to England he had become a lawyer and entered the service of Cardinal Wolsey 'who, perceiving his talents and industry, and finding him ready at all things, evil or good took him into his service'. Cromwell's rise to prominence showed great ambition and, at the fall of Wolsey, he was seen lamenting his fate by another member of the household, complaining, with tears in his eyes that 'I am like to lose all that I have toiled for all the days of my life, for doing my master true and diligent service'. In spite of his fears, Cromwell survived, going on his own initiative to Henry and promising him that, if he employed him, he would make him the richest king that England had ever had. At first, Cromwell was forced to share his power with Anne Boleyn and other members of the court but, by 1539, he was pre-eminent and, with the dissolution of the monasteries, had been as good as his word in making Henry vastly wealthy.

Cromwell's power caused jealousy among the other members of Henry's court. In particular, he had a rival in Stephen Gardiner, Bishop of Winchester. Gardiner was an ardent religious traditionalist and later gained notoriety as Mary I's Lord Chancellor. In October 1535 he was appointed as Henry's ambassador to France and spent the next three years at the French court. Gardiner and Cromwell were implacably opposed and during Gardiner's stay in France Cromwell took steps to politically isolate his rival. Upon his return to England, it took Gardiner some time to re-establish himself and, in August 1539, he suffered a further setback when Cromwell managed to engineer his expulsion from the king's council due to the bishop's dispute with Cromwell's ally, Robert Barnes. This angered Gardiner and, by early 1540, he was looking for revenge against both Cromwell and Barnes.

In 1553 while speaking to the Spanish ambassador, Simon Renard, about another royal match, Gardiner told Renard that:

> It was a dangerous matter to take a share in the marriage of princes, when Cromwell, who arranged the match between the late King Henry and the daughter of Cleves because he believed that Germany would ever afterwards assist this country for her sake; whereas the marriage only lasted one night and ruined Cromwell. Therefore he did not intend to take such a share in the present negotiation as might later bring blame upon him.

There is no doubt then that Gardiner, who was a witness to the events of Anne's brief marriage, considered it to have been the cause of Cromwell's ruin. He was not the only one and, in a letter written in 1541, the religious reformer, Richard Hilles, wrote of Cromwell's fall that 'it was commonly said by most persons, and with great probability, that the real cause of his execution was, that he did not support the king, as Winchester and the other courtiers did, in his project of a divorce, but rather asserted that it would neither be for the king's honour, nor for the good of the kingdom'. Many people saw the king's dislike of Anne as the beginning of the end for Cromwell and this, along with Henry's love for Catherine Howard, provided Gardiner with the opportunity to attack Cromwell's ally, Dr Barnes.

Barnes was well known for his reformist religious views and he had previously been accused of heresy and examined by Cardinal Wolsey. He had travelled widely in Europe and was an associate of Martin Luther and Anne's brother-in-law, John Frederick. For Gardiner, Barnes was a heretic and he made the first move against his rival on the first Sunday in Lent in 1540, preaching at Paul's Cross at a time that Barnes had been appointed to speak. In his sermon, Gardiner made no secret of his distaste for the views of the religious reformers, attacking one of the main tenets of their beliefs, that of justification by faith. As Gardiner hoped he would, Barnes rose to the bait, taking to the same pulpit two weeks later. According to *Hall's Chronicle*, Barnes:

> Beeyng vexed with the Bishoppes Doctrine, he used many tauntes against hym, but one specially whiche was this, that he said if the Bishoppe and he, wer together in Rome with the Pope, he knewe that greate sommes of money, could not save his life, but for the Bishoppe, there was no feare, but that a little intreataunce, should purchase favour enough for hym: By this he noted the Bishop to bee but a Papist.

Gardiner displayed righteous indignation at this attack and went immediately to the king to complain. For Henry, such an open attack on one of his bishops was outrageous and he ordered Barnes to publicly recant his Protestant beliefs. In the week after Easter, Barnes and two of his friends, Drs Jerome and Garrett, made a public recantation in Gardiner's presence, asking forgiveness of him. Gardiner appeared to grant this to his rival, but it was 'a counterfeat forgevenes'. The recantations were not, in any event, sufficient for Henry and, soon afterwards, the three men were sent to the Tower. They were burned as heretics at Smithfield on 30 June, alongside three Catholics who were hanged, drawn and quartered for asserting the supremacy of the pope. It is a mark of Henry's own unique religious opinions that he was able to persecute both Protestants and Catholics. The imprisonment of Barnes was a triumph for Gardiner against Cromwell and the minister was able to do nothing to help his friend.

Gardiner was not Cromwell's only enemy in 1540: Catherine Howard's uncle, the Duke of Norfolk, was also plotting against him. Norfolk and Cromwell had previously co-operated with each other. In early 1538, for example, Norfolk had informed both Henry and Cromwell that he planned to ask them to be godfathers for his eldest grandson. In spite of this, Norfolk's traditional beliefs made it impossible for him to work fully with the more reform minded Cromwell and, with the possibility of another niece sitting on the throne in exchange for Cromwell's candidate, Norfolk was willing to act against him. Norfolk and Cromwell also quarrelled in June 1539 and, while they continued to work together, resentment festered. Norfolk found himself in favour with the king early in 1540 and he was sent as Henry's ambassador to France in February of that year. He was instructed to pursue an alliance with Francis and it is possible that he was informed by the French king that the price of this alliance was the fall of Cromwell. Certainly, Francis had little love for the minister. An alliance with France was exactly what Henry needed if he was to risk offending Anne's brother by rejecting his new wife.

It has been recently suggested that Cromwell was not the advocate of the religious reform that he is usually portrayed to be and that, in fact, he favoured the king's middle of the road approach to the church. To a certain extent this is accurate and Cromwell never openly displayed religious beliefs at variance with the king's. However, he certainly associated with those involved in the religious reform such as Anne Boleyn and Thomas Cranmer. As the architect of the Cleves marriage, Cromwell was aware of the euphoria with which it was greeted in England by the reformers, with one reformer writing in February 1540 that 'the word is powerfully preached by an individual named Barnes, and his fellow-ministers. Books of every kind may be safely exposed to sale'. Henry's sudden interest in the religious beliefs of Barnes and other reformers shows his concern at the religious differences in his kingdom and it is not impossible that, even at that early stage, he had become convinced that Cromwell was responsible for the difficulties in his church.

Cromwell was noticeably in difficulties in early April and Marillac recorded that 'within few days there will be seen in this country a great change in many things; which this king begins to make in his ministers, recalling those he has rejected and degrading those he had raised and Cromwell is tottering'. The new councillors, who included Gardiner and the Bishops of Durham and Bath, were Cromwell's enemies and Marillac saw the minister's fall as imminent. It was therefore a surprise to nearly everyone when, on 18 April, almost without warning, the king appointed Cromwell as Earl of Essex and Grand Chamberlain of England, carrying out the ceremony in front of the whole court. Henry's motives have often been debated with one commentator stating that some suspected it was 'all an artifice, to make people conclude that he must have been a most wicked traitor, and guilty of treason in every possible way; or else the king would never have executed one who was so dear to him, as was made manifest by the presents he had bestowed upon him'. It is probable that Henry, used to turning to Cromwell for delivery of his will, used the honours bestowed on his minister as a way of demonstrating his continued confidence in him, providing, of course, he could accomplish the thing Henry most desired, a divorce from Anne of Cleves.

Soon after Anne and Henry's marriage, when the king's dislike for his bride became clear, Cromwell sought to deflect the blame from himself by turning on the Earl of Southampton who had so praised Anne in Calais. According to Southampton's own report:

> At which tyme therle of Essex calling the said Erle of Southampton to hym, layd sore to his charge, that he had so moch praysed the Quene by his letters from Calise, declaring therby his malicious purpose, how he entended to take occasion to do displeasure to the said Erle, and to turn al the king's miscontentment upon the shulders of the said Erle of Southampton. Upon whom the said Erle of Southampton answered, that he thought his prayse to good purpose, if he could have done any good by it, the mattier being so far passed.

By early June, Cromwell knew that the price of his survival was to secure the king his divorce. On 6 or 7 June, Thomas Wriothesley, one of the king's secretaries, came to Cromwell's house in London. When Cromwell saw

Wriothesley he demanded: 'Have we any newys?' Wriothesley shook his head, saying: 'None, Sir.' Wriothesley then asked Cromwell if he had any business for him to carry out, to which Cromwell replied: 'Nay, I have no business now: but one thyng resteth in my hedd, which troubbleth me, and I thought to tel it you. The king, quoth he, liketh not the Quene, ne did ever like her from the begynnyng. Insomuch as I think adsuredly she be yet as good a mayd for hym as she was whan she came to England.' Wriothesley was stunned by the news and responded: 'Marie, Sir, I am right sory that his Majesty should be so troubled: for Goddes sake devyse how his Grace may be releved by one way or other.' Cromwell asked Wriothesley how this could be achieved and Wriothesley was unable to provide an answer, merely saying that he thought some way could be found. Cromwell shook his head saying 'Wel, wel, it is a great mattier' before Wriothesley departed. The following day Wriothesley went once again to Cromwell and pleaded with him 'for Goddes sake devyse for the relefe of the king; for if he remain in his gref and trouble, we shal al one day smart for it. If his Grace be quiet, we shal have our parts with hym'. Cromwell agreed, saying once again that it was a great matter. When Wriothesley begged him for a remedy Cromwell broke off, troubled.

The end for Cromwell came sooner than he could ever have imagined. On 10 June 1540, as he was leaving the parliament building to go to dinner, a sudden gust of wind blew Cromwell's hat from his head, causing it to fall to the ground. Usually, when a gentleman lost his hat, it was the custom of everyone to doff theirs as a mark of respect. As Cromwell bent to retrieve his hat none of the assembled lords moved to doff their own hats and Cromwell commented drily: 'A high wind indeed must it have been to blow my bonnet off and keep all yours on.' The lords pretended not to hear him and they all went to dinner together. During the meal no one spoke to the minister.

Once the meal was over, the lords moved to the council chamber to carry out the business of the day. As usual, Cromwell sat by the window to hear petitioners for an hour before joining his fellow counsellors. When he reached them he discovered that they were already seated and commented: 'You were in a great hurry, gentlemen, to get seated.' Again, no one answered him but as he went to sit in his usual chair Norfolk called out: 'Cromwell, do not sit there; that is no place for thee. Traitors do not sit amongst gentlemen.' Cromwell was furious and responded: 'I am not a traitor.' As he spoke, the captain of the guard entered and grabbed him by the arm, informing the astonished minister that he was arresting him. When Cromwell asked what the charge was, he was told he would find out later. Cromwell then asked to see Henry but this was refused. As Cromwell was led from the room he was subjected to one final indignity as Norfolk cried out: 'Stop, captain, traitors must not wear the Garter,' before ripping Cromwell's badge from his chest. The minister was hustled out of a back door of the palace to a waiting boat and taken to the Tower while the council continued their business.

Cromwell's arrest came suddenly and it stunned much of the court. Only Thomas Cranmer dared to speak for his friend, writing to the king that:

> I heard yesterday in your grace's council, that he [Cromwell] is a traitor: yet who cannot be sorrowful and amazed that he should be a traitor against your Majesty, he that was so advanced by your Majesty; he whose surety was only by your Majesty; he who loved your Majesty (as I ever thought) no less than God; he who studied always to set forwards whatsoever way your majesty's will and pleasure; he that cared for no man's displeasure to serve your majesty; he that was such a servant, in my judgment, in wisdom, diligence, faithfulness, and experience, as no prince in this realm ever had.

Cranmer continued saying: 'I loved him as my friend, for so I took him to be.' However, he then added, in order to ensure that his own position was not jeopardised, that 'now, if he be a traitor, I am sorry that ever I loved him or trusted him'. With his arrest, Cromwell's condemnation was a foregone conclusion and, in an irony not lost on his contemporaries, he was denied a trial, instead being condemned by an Act of Attainder, a process that he himself had brought into law.

The crimes of which Cromwell was accused were extensive and they were intended to fully blacken his reputation. Following his arrest there were rumours that he had planned to make himself king by marrying

Princess Mary and, while this charge was not included in the Attainder, many other outrageous accusations were. In the Attainder, Cromwell was accused both of treason against the king and of being the most extreme form of heretic, a Sacramentary. In the Attainder it was claimed that Cromwell's heresy had led him into treason and that, in answer to the condemnation of Barnes, he had stated of the religious reform that 'if the king would turn from it, yet I would not turn; and if the king did turn and all his people I would fight in the field in my own person with my sword in my hand against him and all other'. If this conversation took place then it was treason indeed. However, Cromwell, who owed his prominent position to the king, is very unlikely to have been a traitor. His main crime was that, in Henry's eyes, he had brought about his marriage to Anne and, even more fundamentally, he had failed to secure the king a divorce.

Cromwell's fall was greeted with rejoicing in London and elsewhere. On the day of Cromwell's arrest, Henry wrote to his ambassador in France asking him to inform Francis. When he heard the news, Francis declared it to be a miracle. On the day of the arrest a great crowd came out to watch as archers surrounded Cromwell's house while the king's officers made an inventory of his goods. The officers were instructed to search, in particular, for anything that could assist in the king's divorce and, on 11 June, they were able to produce several letters both received and sent by Cromwell to the Lutheran lords of Germany. It is not recorded what these papers were but, according to Marillac, they threw the king into a rage and he vowed that he would 'abolish all memory of him as the greatest wretch ever born in England'. He also insisted that the minister should no longer be known by his titles or offices and, instead, referred to as simply 'Thomas Cromwell, shearman' as a reference to his humble birth.

While the content of the German documents is not recorded, it is clear that they were considered helpful in any divorce. Henry also had plans to make use of the minister in the matter and he sent word to Cromwell that he required a full account of everything that had happened since Anne's arrival in England. Cromwell knew that this was his only chance of survival and he set out everything in great detail, beginning:

1. Anne of Cleves by Hans Holbein. The portrait that convinced Henry that Anne was the wife for him.

2. Anne of Cleves. Anne looks pleasing enough in both surviving portraits although her elaborate German clothes drew critical comments when she arrived in England.

3. Anne of Cleves.

4. Sibylla of Cleves. Anne's elder sister was a famous beauty and it was hoped by everyone in England that Anne would resemble her.

Opposite: 5. Henry VIII at around the time of his marriage to Anne. The king was already elderly and overweight and his hat conceals his baldness.

6. Mary of Hungary. The Regent of the Netherlands was instructed by her brother the Emperor to negotiate with Henry for the marriage of her niece, Christina of Denmark, but she was always opposed to the match.

7. Christina of Denmark, Duchess of Milan by Hans Holbein. Christina's portrait enchanted Henry and she became his first choice as his fourth wife.

8. Christina of Denmark as Duchess of Milan. Christina was said to be beautiful and her choice of a French hood on the medal would have pleased the king.

9. Emperor Charles V. Charles was prepared to negotiate with Henry for the hand of his niece, Christina of Denmark, but, as the nephew of Henry's first wife, Catherine of Aragon, he was not enthusiastic about allying his family once again to the king through marriage.

10. Francis I of France. Francis offered a number of brides to Henry but his real interest lay in an alliance with Charles V.

Above: 11. Deal Castle, Kent. Anne visited the fortress upon landing in England in order to refresh herself for the journey ahead.

Below: 12. Dover Castle, Kent. Anne spent her first night in England at the castle.

Opposite: 13. Catherine Willoughby, Duchess of Suffolk. The Duchess met Anne at Deal Castle in order to escort her to London.

Dutcheſs of Suffolk.

14. Thomas Cranmer on his memorial at Oxford. Cranmer met Anne outside Canterbury in order to escort her in to the city and he was dismayed by the small company that turned out to greet her there.

Below: 15. Canterbury Cathedral. Anne spent her third night in England being entertained in the city by the Archbishop.

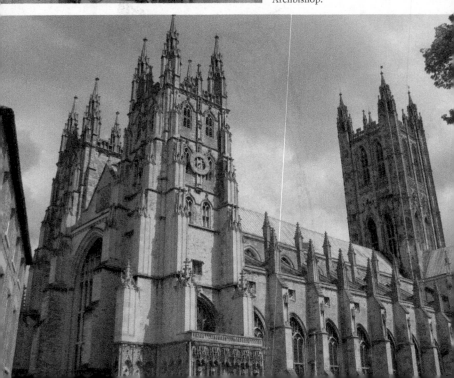

16. St Augustine's Abbey, Canterbury. Little remains of the royal apartments in which Anne stayed on her journey to London.

18. A portrait miniature of a younger Henry VIII.

19. Jane Seymour. The death of Henry's third wife in childbirth left Henry once again the most eligible bachelor in Europe.

Left page: 17. Henry VIII at King's College, Cambridge. The king is portrayed magnificently but, by 1540, the physical reality was very different.

20. Henry VIII in later life. Anne was faced with the prospect of the most terrifying husband in England and the fact that she survived her marriage is testament to her good sense and pragmatic approach.

Opposite: 21. Edward VI as Prince of Wales. Edward's birth in 1537 was Henry's dearest wish but one son was not enough and it was hoped that Anne would quickly provide a Duke of York.

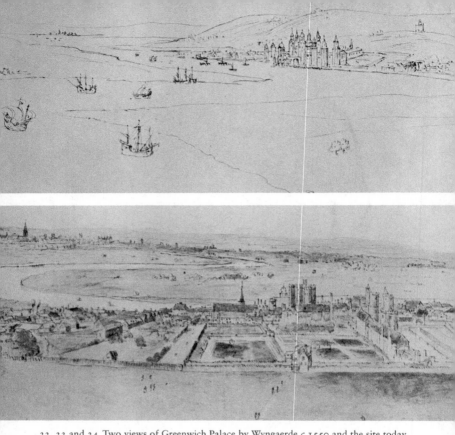

22, 23 and 24 Two views of Greenwich Palace by Wyngaerde *c.*1550 and the site today. Nothing remains of the Tudor palace but the site of Anne's official reception and welcome to England in front of the palace remains relatively unchanged.

Opposite: 25. Costume Designs by Hans Holbein. Anne's heavy German fashions were mocked upon her arrival to England where less elaborate clothes were favoured.

26. Thomas Cromwell. Cromwell was the architect of Anne's marriage and it ultimately cost him his head.

27. Thomas Howard, Duke of Norfolk. The uncle of Catherine Howard helped to coach Catherine in her relationship with the king.

28 and 29. Two views of Richmond Palace, first by Hollar *c.*1650 and in a later engraving. Anne was sent to the palace on the pretext of avoiding the plague but she quickly came to realize that her separation from Henry was due to a more sinister purpose.

30 and 31. Richmond Palace today. Little now remains of the fine Tudor palace that Anne used as her main residence during the early years of her divorce.

32. A Pageant Design for Anne Boleyn's Coronation by Holbein. Anne of Cleves expected a similarly grand coronation but all plans were quietly abandoned after her first meeting with the king.

Opposite: 33. Anne Boleyn by Holbein. Anne of Cleves was terrified that she would suffer the same fate as her unfortunate predecessor.

Top: 34. Little now remains of Anne's second residence Bletchingley Palace and an archway from the building has been incorporated into a more modern building.

Right: 35. Catherine of Aragon. Henry VIII's first wife was exiled from London and mistreated following her divorce and Anne was anxious to ensure that the same did not happen to her.

36. Anne of Cleves' House, Lewes. Anne received the house as part of her divorce settlement and the rental income helped ensure that she was a woman of independent means.

37. The fine gardens at Anne of Cleves' House, Lewes. The house is now open as a museum.

38. The Priest's House, West Hoathly, Sussex. Anne received the house as part of her divorce settlement.

39. Hever Castle, Kent. Anne was granted the home of the Boleyn family by the king and used it as one of her main residences after his death.

40. Anne's signature. Following her divorce Anne always tactfully signed herself as 'Anna, the daughter of Cleves'.

41. Catherine Howard. Catherine was the youngest and prettiest of Henry's wives and Anne was unable to compete with her.

42. Princess Mary. Anne enjoyed a firm friendship with Henry's eldest daughter who was less than a year younger than her.

Opposite: 43. Catherine Howard as the Queen of Sheba in a window at King's College Chapel, Cambridge. Anne blamed Henry's infatuation with Catherine for the failure of her marriage.

48. Bletchingley Church. Once Cawarden had acquired Bletchingley from Anne he immediately set about ensuring that the church conformed to his Protestant ideals.

49. Mary I. Anne and Mary enjoyed a strong friendship but the queen distanced herself from her former stepmother following Wyatt's Rebellion.

Opposite: 50. Philip II of Spain. Anne wrote to congratulate Mary on her marriage to Philip but she was disappointed by the marriage, favouring the Archduke Ferdinand.

51 and 52 Elizabeth I. Anne was fond of her younger stepdaughter but the association was to have unfortunate consequences during the reign of Mary I.

53 and 54
Westminster Abbey.
Anne was given a
royal funeral in the
Abbey and she lies
in an elaborate tomb
there, paid for by
Mary I.

Moste gracious king and most mercyfull souerayng your most humble most obbesyand and most bounden subiett and most lamentable seruaunt and prisoner prostrate at the feate of your most excellent magestye haue herd your pleasure by the mouthe of your comptroller which was that I sholde wrytte to your most excellent highness such things as I thought mete to be wryttyn con` consernyng my most miserable state and condicyon for the whiche your most haboundaunt goodness benignyte and lycens.

Cromwell's letters proved useful to the king but they were not enough to save him and, on 28 July 1540, he was led out of the Tower to be executed. On the scaffold, Cromwell made a speech asking forgiveness but denying that he died a heretic. He then knelt down and prayed before being executed 'by a ragged and butcherly miser, who very ungodly performed the office'.

Anne had no idea of just what information Cromwell had been asked for, or of the documents that were felt to be so important to her marriage. Long before Cromwell's execution, events in her marriage were spiralling beyond her control. Cromwell's account of the marriage provided the king with some of the evidence that he needed to begin divorce proceedings and this, along with the assurance of Francis's friendship which the arrest of Cromwell brought, gave him the confidence to take action. Just after midsummer's day, while Cromwell was still languishing in the Tower in the hope of reprieve, Anne received word from the king that her household was to move to Richmond Palace. The official reason was to ensure that she was safely out of the way of the plague in London but Anne, and everyone else at court, knew that the threat of plague was no greater than usual. On 26 June 1540 Anne summoned her brother's ambassador to complain of her treatment and, while he sought to reassure her that Richmond was not very far from court, Anne told him, ominously, that she knew very well what had happened to Catherine of Aragon and that there were rumours in the city that Henry would discard her for a lady-in-waiting, just as he had done with his first wife.

10

Pretended Matrimony: 6 July – 28 July 1540

Anne's removal to Richmond was the first step taken by Henry towards divorce. When intent on ending his previous marriages, the king had always made a point of keeping the soon-to-be discarded wife out of his sight.

Towards the end of June 1540, a memorandum written in Gardiner's own hand shows the means by which Henry meant to proceed. Investigations into the marriage were to be carried out secretly and it was agreed that Anne's precontract with Francis of Lorraine would be investigated. Gardiner also noted that it was necessary 'to consider to what sort the king's [majesty's Council] shall cause the matter to be opened unto the queen, and by whom and when and [where]'. It was also agreed that Cromwell, who was then still in the Tower awaiting death, would be examined on the matter. Proof would be gathered to demonstrate Henry's unwillingness to go through with the marriage together with evidence that the marriage was not consummated. Anne's confession of this was also to be used 'if it may be attained'.

One area to be examined was the renunciation of Anne's betrothal to Francis of Lorraine. The day before the wedding, William's ambassadors had promised to supply a copy of the renunciation and, in February 1540, they supplied a copy of a notarial certificate stating that the betrothal had been broken off in 1535. This document was stamped with a seal in the shape of a beer pot and was instantly seized upon as dubious. As Gardiner wrote in his memorandum 'the instrument signed with the bere pot containeth no m[anner] of discharge at all, but rather ministereth matter of m[uch] doubt'.

Henry also instructed his ambassador in France to secretly approach Francis of Lorraine's uncle, the powerful Cardinal of Lorraine, and ask him about the betrothal and, in particular, 'if there be any cloud in the matter, we should be glad to have it cleared'. The document signed with the beer pot merely stated that on 15 February 1535 Charles of Egmond, Duke of Guelders had noted that the marriage was no longer going ahead. It is likely that, by 1540, the prospect of Anne's marriage had become so remote that the necessary documents simply no longer existed in Cleves. However, for Henry, the uncertainty over Anne's marital status was a godsend.

Anne did not have a clear idea about what was happening in the early days of July 1540 and the language barrier was a particular difficulty. Anne had been in England for over six months and, with Mistress Gilmyn's tuition before her arrival, she must have acquired a good working knowledge of the language by July but she was by no means fluent. Her Chancellor, Rutland, admitted on 6 July, he still required an interpreter to speak to her, commenting of Anne and of her brother's ambassador that 'I understand neither of them'. She was isolated in her own household and it was a terrible shock when she first received word of Henry's intentions.

In order for Anne and Henry's marriage to be investigated by a church court, it was necessary for the king to obtain Anne's consent. In the early hours of the morning of 6 July a messenger arrived from the king to tell Anne of his concerns over their marriage. Anne immediately summoned her brother's ambassador, Carl Harst, and the pair sat together in her apartments for some time while Anne digested the news. Some time after four o'clock in the morning, Anne sent for Rutland who arrived with Wymond Carew, another member of Anne's household, to act as interpreter. The news of what the king intended struck Anne into speechlessness and Harst spoke to Rutland, telling him that Henry had sent the queen a message that required an answer. According to Rutland:

I advised her accordingly to send awnswer ether by writing or by mothe as she pleased. Whereupon she determined to send Berd by cause he brought the message, and she wold not write, and again the Imbassador wold not go of the message by no mene. Wherfor Berd cumys again with the awnswer by mothe. And for that I dyd see her to take the matter hevely, I desired her to be of good comfort, and that the kynges highness ys so gracious and wertues a prince that he would nothing but that shuld stond with the law of God and for the discharge of his conscience and hers and the quyetnes of this realme hereafter, and at the sute of all his lords and commyns which ys the state of the hole realme, his highness [is conte]nt to refar the matter to the bysshoppes and the clergye who be as well lerned men and of as good conscience and lyveyng as any be in the world, so that her grace hath cause to reyose and not to be sorry, whiche matter she hard well and sayd nothing to yt.

It is clear from Rutland's letter that he was already well acquainted with the king's plans and his words were the official line, meant to stop Anne causing a scene. As he noted, Anne took the matter 'heavily' and, while she is normally portrayed by historians to have taken the divorce well and to have been unconcerned, in reality, Anne was terrified.

Anne had known Henry's frightening marital history before she arrived in England and, like Christina of Milan, was well acquainted with the rumours that Henry had ordered his first wife to be poisoned, executed his second and caused the third to die of neglect following childbirth. Anne of Cleves had known for months that something was badly wrong in her marriage but she cannot have imagined that Henry would move so quickly against her. When Henry's messenger arrived in the middle of the night Anne must have feared imminent imprisonment in the Tower, as had happened to Anne Boleyn. She therefore meekly agreed to have the marriage investigated, clinging to the hope that it was merely the formality that the king suggested and that, in reality, he did not mean to rid himself of her.

If Anne was terrified at the news, her brother's ambassador, Carl Harst, was bewildered and furious. He refused point blank to take the message of Anne's acquiescence to the king or to be involved in the investigation of the marriage in any way. For Harst, it was an outrage that Anne, a noble daughter of a German duke, should be treated in such a way. As soon as it was morning, Harst stormed up to the court, leaving Anne alone with a household that she was suddenly aware she might not be able to trust. At court, Harst was sent for by Norfolk, Cranmer, Sir Anthony Browne and the Bishop of Durham who apologized that, as an oversight, they had not invited him to lunch. This casual concern about the ambassador's dining arrangements threw him slightly and he was further confused by the Bishop of Durham's reassurances that there were some rumours going around the common people surrounding the legitimacy of the marriage and that, in order to be sure and to avoid bloodshed in the future, the king had ordered the marriage to be tried. He was assured that Anne would continue to be treated as befitted her station. Harst was left requesting that matters be delayed until ambassadors from William and John Frederick could arrive from Germany but the bishop merely brushed aside his concerns, refusing to tell him anything further. At the end of the meeting the bishop assured him that Henry was friendly towards Anne and that he would probably keep her whatever happened. Harst went away, thoroughly confused and convinced that the king and his council were working against Anne.

Anne had a lonely wait at Richmond and she stayed close with her remaining German servants, aware that any of the English servants could be an enemy. Soon after the arrival of the first messenger, she received a visit from Thomas Audeley, Henry's Lord Chancellor, and Gardiner. The content of this visit is not recorded but it may have been an attempt to persuade Anne to confess to the non-consummation of her marriage. The visitors were able to get nothing from Anne and she was so upset that she immediately sent a servant to Harst to ask him to return to her. Audeley and Gardiner did not leave empty handed, obtaining a deposition from three of Anne's ladies recording their claims to have spoken to Anne some time before about her ignorance of sexual matters. As already discussed, this conversation is highly unlikely to have occurred but, in the absence of Anne's express confession, it was the best that the two men could obtain.

Both Anne and Harst were caught unawares by the speed at which matters were moving and Anne, far from home in a foreign country, relied heavily on the ambassador for advice. He was furious to find that Anne had been approached by the councillors while he was not there and, once again, he travelled to court to complain about the 'unjust interrogations' of the queen. He complained that the councillors had gone so swiftly to Anne that he had been unable to attend. He also asked, furiously, whether it was the custom in England for a queen of such high status as Anne to be found and then got rid of on a whim. He demanded that the king be approached by the council, apparently unable to believe that the king could have sanctioned such treatment of Anne. Anne, on the other hand, knew her husband and his reputation well enough to understand that what was happening came only from him, and she was devastated.

While Harst moved backwards and forwards between Richmond and the court, Anne waited quietly in her apartments. Henry always claimed to Anne and the wider world that he had consented to the investigation of the marriage at the request of parliament and it was they who were concerned about the succession in the event that Anne bore a son. This was a fiction, as Anne knew, and the last men who had dared stand in the way of Henry's matrimonial desires, Thomas More and Bishop John Fisher, had lost their heads for this opposition. Parliament would never have dared raise the matter unless its members had received a strong indication that this was what the king expected. Henry responded quickly to their petition, granting a commission to the clergy to investigate the marriage on 6 July.

As soon as Anne's consent to the investigation of her marriage had been obtained, a convocation of the leading clergy was summoned at Westminster. Henry's commission was read and Gardiner made a speech, setting out the arguments against the marriage. The assembled clergymen reviewed the evidence and, in what was a foregone conclusion, agreed at 3 o'clock in the afternoon of 7 July that 'the king and Anne of Cleves were nowise bound by the marriage solemnised between them, and it was decreed to send letters testimonial of this to the king'. Anne was offered no advocate for the convocation and no one presented her position, or any evidence in support of the marriage. She was almost certainly not aware that the convocation was sitting so soon; if she had been, Harst would doubtless have attempted to force his way into the Chapter House.

The evidence used by Henry to prove the invalidity of the marriage was threefold. The first was Anne's betrothal to Francis of Lorraine. This was a convenient method to invalidate the marriage but it was not the only evidence used and the convocation's ruling that both Henry and Anne were free to marry as they chose demonstrates that there was still a question mark over just whether Anne was bound to Francis or not.

The second cause for the invalidity of the marriage was Henry's lack of consent to the marriage. In order to support this position, he had gathered depositions from members of his council and privy chamber to recount their memories of his first meeting with Anne and their subsequent marriage. Henry's brother-in-law, the Duke of Suffolk, reported that the king had never wanted to marry Anne. Lord Russell went further, claiming that the king had often lamented the marriage to him and he had perceived from Henry's 'fashion and maner, that he hath ben nothing content with this marriage, but always troubled and unquiet therin'. Sir Anthony Browne stated that the king 'did never in his hart favour the lady to mary her, if outward respects had not enforced him to that act'. Henry was so desperate to rid himself of Anne and marry his new beloved, Catherine Howard, that he provided his own deposition, declaring that 'I never for love to the woman consented to marry; nor yet if she brought maidenhead with her, took any from her by true carnal copulation'.

This statement was the basis of the third argument used to show the invalidity of the marriage: lack of consummation. While the other two grounds could usefully be used in the invalidity of the marriage, this, if the king could prove it, was the strongest cause for an annulment and even Thomas Cromwell, languishing in the Tower was instructed to write confirming his conversations with his master on the subject. Henry, his doctors and a number of members of his court provided evidence to assert this, with Sir Thomas Hennege, for example claiming that Henry had informed him that the marriage was not consummated and that he believed 'the queen, for any part of the king's body, to be yet as good a mayd as ever she was'. In the absence of Anne's own declaration on the subject, the report of Anne's ladies claiming that she had not known what consummation meant was also used.

Henry was anxious that Anne would swear that the marriage had been consummated and there is evidence that, if that occurred, his mood would quickly have turned as sour as it had done with Catherine of Aragon when she had opposed divorce. According to Herbert, there were other areas that could be used to prove the invalidity of the marriage, which he referred to as 'secret causes'. According to Herbert, of these 'secret causes', 'the king without great necessity would not have disclos'd, because they touch'd the honour of the lady'. While these 'secret causes' are not mentioned in the official record of the trial they almost certainly related to the king's doubts about Anne's virginity at the time of their marriage. Following their first night together he had claimed that she was no virgin and his own comments that he left her as good a maid as he found her demonstrate his beliefs in that area. The divorce of Henry and Catherine of Aragon had descended to arguments of whether or not she was a virgin when the king married her and Henry would have been prepared to go to the same level if necessary with Anne. Anne was certainly a virgin at the time of her marriage, but reports to the contrary could have been damaging. Anne was never made aware of Henry's doubts about her virginity but it is certain that, had she not acquiesced so quickly, the king would have used them.

Soon after the verdict had been given, Henry sent further commissioners to Anne at Richmond to obtain her agreement to the annulment. According to the commissioners, Anne took the news well, and, when they spoke to her through an interpreter, she, 'without alteracion of countenance hath made answer, th'affecte wherof tendith to this, that she is content always with your Majestie'. Anne may have appeared collected to the commissioners but when she heard the news of her divorce she was terrified. According to Herbert, upon the arrival of the commissioners, Anne fainted. Once she had recovered from her swoon, she exhibited great anxiety. Harst had spoken to Anne shortly before the commissioners arrived and told her to have patience. Anne insisted that she had given herself to one man and she kept him as her husband and they could never divorce until the bitter death. According to Harst, Anne cried and screamed bitterly about her situation and it broke his heart to hear her. This was never communicated to the commissioners and, because of the need to use an interpreter, they misinterpreted Anne's quiet demeanour in their presence as acceptance.

For Anne, the matter was clear; she was Henry's wife and she would be so until death separated them. At the same time however, she was alone in England and Harst does not appear to have been present when the commissioners were with her. Anne apparently feared that she would be executed, as Anne Boleyn had been, if she resisted the king. When she heard that if she accepted the divorce she would be favourably treated, she was so relieved that she agreed, fearful that worse would befall her if she disobeyed. She agreed to write to the king confirming her acceptance of all that happened. She began speaking of Henry's doubts over the marriage and the need for it to be examined by the clergy before continuing:

> It may please you majesty to know that, though this case must needs be most hard and sorrowful unto me, for the great love which I bear to your most noble person, yet, having more regard to God and his trust than to any worldly affection, as it beseemed me, at the beginning, to submit me to such examination and determination of the said clergy, whom I have and do accept for judges competent in that behalf. So now being ascertained how the same clergy hath therein given their judgement and sentence, I knowledge myself hereby to accept and approve the same, wholly and entirely putting myself, for my state and condition, to your highness' goodness and pleasure; most humbly beseeching your Majesty that, though it be determined that the pretended matrimony between us is void and of none effect, whereby I neither can nor will repute myself your Grace's wife, considering this sentence (whereunto I stand) and your Majesty's clean and pure living with me, yet it will please you to take me for one of your most humble servants, and so to determine of me, as I may sometimes have the fruition of your most noble presence; which as I shall esteem for a great benefit, so, my lords and others of your Majesty's council, now being with me, have put me in comfort thereof; and that your highness will take me for your sister; for the which I most humbly thank you accordingly.

Anne signed her letter as 'Anne, the daughter of Cleves' in a final confirmation of her changed status. Anne, unlike Catherine of Aragon, had no child whose position would be affected by the divorce and, after only six months, she was very far from being in love with Henry. In spite of her opposition to the divorce, she knew that she had no option but to agree and that the king could make her life very difficult if she disobeyed.

Henry was amazed to find Anne apparently so willing to agree to the invalidity of their marriage and he wrote back to her immediately to express his gratitude towards her:

> Right dear and right entirely beloved sister,
> By the relation of the lord Master, lord Privy Seal and others of our Council lately addressed unto you we perceive the continuance of your conformity, which before was reported, and by your letters is eftsoons testified. We take your wise and honourable proceedings therein in most thankful part, as it is done in respect of God and his trust, and, continuing your conformity, you shall find in us a perfect friend, content to repute you as our dearest sister. We shall, within five or six days, when our Parliament ends, determine your state after such honourable sort as you shall have good cause to be content, we minding to endow you with £4000 of yearly revenue. We have appointed you two houses, that at Richmond where you now lie, and the other at Blechinglegh, not far from London that you may be near us and, as you desire, able to repair to our court to see us, as we shall repair to you. When Parliament ends, we shall, in passing, see and speak with you, and you shall more largely see what a friend you and your friends have of us. Be quiet and merry.

Anne's reluctant agreement to the divorce not only pleased, but also surprised, the king, who was still under the impression that he was the handsome young prince of his youth, writing to his ambassadors in Cleves that when Anne heard of the divorce she was at first troubled and perplexed due to the 'great love and affection which she seemed to have only to our person'.

Henry was determined to be generous to Anne both in gratitude for her quick acceptance of the inevitable and in the hope of retaining her brother's friendship. He sent his letter with Suffolk, Southampton and Sir Thomas Wriothesley on 12 July to Anne in order to agree the divorce settlement with her. The commissioners gave Anne the letter and a token of money as soon as they arrived which Anne received 'very humbly' and asked them to read it to her. The commissioners however insisted that she read it herself with an interpreter and they left the room while Anne and her interpreter read through the terms offered by the king. Henry was indeed generous and he offered to officially adopt Anne as his sister, giving her precedence over all other ladies at court save his subsequent wives and his daughters. He also offered the generous annual income set out in his letter as well the two palaces, hangings, plate and furniture, jewels and a household made up of 'a good number of officers, the heads being noble'. The final grant of lands to Anne would not be made until January 1541 but it left her wealthy indeed, providing her with properties such as the house in Lewes, Sussex now known as Anne of Cleves' House. It was intended that most of the property would be let by Anne in order to provide her with an income but Richmond and Bletchingley were intended to become her homes. Anne already knew and liked Richmond but the mention of Bletchingley raised her suspicions that she was to be exiled from court as Catherine of Aragon had been and she recalled the commissioners to demand where Bletchingley was. Once Anne had been reassured, she readily accepted the settlement, amazed and grateful at what was being done. She made only one request for herself: that Henry's younger daughter, Elizabeth, of whom she had become fond, would be allowed to visit her occasionally, a request that was granted.

In spite of her agreement to the settlement, Anne was not prepared to agree to everything Henry wanted. The commissioners had been instructed by Henry to obtain a letter from Anne to her brother, setting out her agreement to the divorce. Although Anne was prepared to go along with Henry in relation to their marriage in order to save her own life and future, she was painfully aware of the humiliating position that she was in and she refused point blank to write, saying:

what, should I write to my brother before he write to me? It were not meet. But when he shall write the King's Gr[ace] shall know what he writeth, and [as he answereth] him so will I answer him with the [best will] and pleasure. And I trust, hows[oever he] or the duke of Saxe take this m[atter, his] Grace will be good to me, for I [remain at] his pleasure.

Anne was under no illusions as to how her family in Germany would take the news and she told the commissioners that she feared her brother would 'slay' her if she returned to Germany. As it turned out, William never blamed Anne for what had happened, knowing Henry's reputation as well as his sister did, but Anne was uncomfortably aware of the shameful position that Henry had put her in.

The commissioners decided not to push the matter with Anne and instead wrote to Henry suggesting that it would be better for her to write to William only when the duke had first written to her as, if she were to breach convention by writing first, it might make 'him think the matter were feared he[re than] otherwise'. Henry was not prepared to rely on Anne's promise, writing that without her letter she might later say that she had agreed ignorantly. Anne held out against the commissioners' requests for some days before finally agreeing to write to her brother.

Anne's letter to her brother was the most difficult that she ever had to write. She had last seen him as she set out triumphantly to make a great marriage and to become a great queen. It was traumatic for her to have to tell her brother of the failure of her marriage but she had no choice. Anne wrote:

My dear and wellbeloved brother. After my most hearty commendations. Where by your letters of the 13th of this month, which I have seen written to the king's Majesty of England, my most dear and kind brother, I do perceive that you take the matter, lately moved and determined between him and me, somewhat to heart. Forasmuch as I had rather you knew the truth by mine advertisement, than, for want thereof, you should be deceived by vain reports, I thought meet to write these present letters unto you, by the which it shall lease you to understand that, being substantially advertised how the nobles and commons of this Realm desired the king's highness to commit the examination of the matter of marriage between his Majesty and me, to the examination and determination of the whole Clergy of this Realm, I did then willingly consent thereunto. And since the determination made, have also, upon intimation of their proceedings, allowed, approved, and agreed unto the same, wherein I had more respect (as beseemed me) to trust than to any worldy affection, that might move me to the contrary. And did the rather condescend thereunto, for that my body remaineth in the integrity which I brought into this realm. And being the matter thus finished, to advertise you how I am used. Surely the king's highness, whom I cannot now justly have, nor will repute, as my husband, hath nevertheless taken and adopted me for his sister, and, as a most kind, loving, and friendly brother useth me, with as much or more humanity and liberality, as you, I myself, or any of our kin or allies, could well wish or desire.

Anne added that she was well satisfied with her treatment and asked that William continue in his friendship towards Henry. She finished saying that 'I purpose to lead my life in this Realm', perhaps already aware that Henry intended to use her as a hostage in England to ensure that he remained on friendly terms with William and John Frederick. Once Anne had written the letter she spoke pleasantly with Olisleger's nephew, who was to take the letter to Cleves. For Anne, writing the letter was something of a release and, later that same day she sent Henry her wedding ring, asking that 'it might be broken in pieces as a thing which she knew of no force or value'.

Henry and Anne's divorce was met with incredulity across Europe. Charles V was perplexed when he heard, asking what the cause of the doubts of the marriage was. Francis I was even more confused asking, when he was informed 'what, with the matrimony made with the queen that now is?' On being informed that this was, indeed the case, Francis simply sighed and became quiet. Among Anne's family the news was received angrily. Anne's sister, Sibylla, refused to accept the divorce, continuing to refer to Anne as Queen of England. Sibylla's husband, John Frederick, was furious and the Schmalkaldic League immediately broke off relations with

England. In late 1544 and early 1545, when Henry again attempted to re-establish links with the League, he was rebuffed with John Frederick refusing to have any dealings with Henry whom he referred to as that 'crazy man'.

Henry knew that his divorce from Anne might lead to a breach with her family in Germany. William had already been informed that the marriage was to be investigated and had written to Henry confirming that 'he would be content with justice'. Henry sent Olisleger's nephew, Florence de Diaceto, whom he had employed as a servant, to Cleves with Anne's letter and, upon reading it, William withdrew to consider the matter further. That evening, Olisleger visited the English ambassadors in Cleves and told them that 'though the Duke was sorry about the chance, he would not depart from his amity with the king'. He continued that William was 'troubled at the lady Anne's remaining there, and asked whether the king could be induced to suffer her to return'. He was told it was Anne's own choice. The following day William answered that 'as far as he knew, there never was any matrimony between the lady and the young Marquis of Lorraine; that he is sorry it is otherwise found, but he trusts the king will order the matter to his honour, and desires to continue the amity and league'. This was the best that Henry could hope for as William refused to give his assent to the divorce. In spite of Anne's concerns about William's reaction, he never blamed her, regretting only that he had ever sent her to England and saying privately that he was glad 'his sister had sped no worse'. He then wrote to Anne, no doubt expressing his condolences, a letter that Anne passed to the king, as she had agreed to do with all her correspondence, who read it and then returned it to her.

For Anne, the weeks surrounding her divorce were a bewildering time. She may have been glad of the public sympathy for her; even in her short time as queen, she had become popular. One contemporary commented that it 'was great pitie that so good a ladie as she is should as sone [have] lost her great joy'. The French ambassador also commented that Anne was to be commended for showing 'patience in affliction'. Public opinion was with Anne and another contemporary complained that 'the king's affections were alienated from the lady Anne to that young girl Catherine'.

'That young girl Catherine' was high in the king's favour in the summer of 1540 and, on 28 July, the very day of Cromwell's execution, Henry married her privately at Oatlands Palace. Henry showed concern for Anne's feelings and, a few days later, he left his new queen to travel with a small company from Hampton Court to Richmond to dine with Anne. Now that they were no longer married, the strained relationship between Henry and Anne disappeared and they talked together merrily. Over dinner Henry informed Anne of his new marriage, something that Anne was expecting. Relieved at her survival and aware that she was now one of the wealthiest people in the kingdom, Anne congratulated the king, showing no evidence of distress.

Despite her acquiescence, Anne always believed herself to be the legitimate wife of the king and the true queen. In spite of this she was, first and foremost, a survivor and, if the price of that survival was a denial of her true status in exchange for a life of opulent retirement, she was prepared to play along, even if that meant accepting a new lower status beside her former maid, Queen Catherine Howard.

That Young Girl Catherine:
28 July 1540 – 12 February 1542

Henry's marriage to 'that young girl Catherine' was not a shock to Anne and she took the news graciously, glad that he had at least had the kindness to tell her in person. In the summer of 1540 Anne's main emotion was relief that she had survived a marriage to Henry VIII and that she had done so well out of the settlement.

Within days of the divorce being pronounced, Henry's commissioners arrived at Richmond to discharge Anne's officers and servants who had been appointed to serve her as queen. At the same time, new attendants and servants arrived to serve Anne as the king's sister, including Katherine Bassett, who had previously been rejected by the king as an attendant of Anne. Though Anne outwardly accepted the changes in her household with good grace, she was not entirely happy with those appointed to serve her. By late August 1540 tensions were already apparent in her household and one of Anne's servants, Wymond Carew, wrote to a member of Henry's council to complain that:

> I pray you learn of my lord Privy Seal whether I and my wife shall have the same allowance as Mr Horssey and his wife have, for I think myself no meaner than he. If his lordship seem not so to esteem me, get my brother Denny to dispatch me hence, for the Lady Anne of Clevelond is bent to do me displeasure. I think she has heard how I procured the knowledge of such letters as were sent to her, which of truth at the beginning she denied. She esteems my wife two degress under Mrs Horssey.

Anne had promised the king that he could view all her correspondence from her family in Cleves but she had no intention of keeping this promise, seeing no reason why her personal correspondence should be read by others. It is understandable that she came to view the unreliable Carew, who was actively spying on her, as an enemy in her household, particularly as, in the same letter, he continued saying that 'she had a letter three days past from her Grace's brother, and because she did not seem minded to send it to the king I asked her brother's ambassador whether she had had any, and he said they were letters of congratulations from her brother'. Carew told Harst to advise Anne to send them to the king for him to read. Anne was furious at this intrusion into her privacy and made a particular point of sending the next few letters to the council herself as a demonstration of her disapproval.

In spite of these intrusions, for the most part, Anne found her first few weeks of independence enjoyable. She remained at Richmond until the end of the year and became fond of the palace, making it her primary residence. The palace had been built by Henry VII between 1497 and 1507. It had been intended to demonstrate the splendour of the Tudor dynasty and had cost the king more than £14,000. As well as a chapel and great hall, there were sumptuous apartments for the king and queen and Anne continued to occupy the queen's apartments as the mistress of the palace. The palace was also surrounded by two parks and luxurious gardens with a banqueting house and tennis court. Henry VIII had spent a great deal of time at Richmond during the early years of his reign but had become jealous of Cardinal Wolsey's even more opulent palace of Hampton Court, forcing the Cardinal to exchange the palace for Richmond. With the Cardinal's fall, Richmond passed back into royal control but Henry was happy to hand it over to Anne. For Anne, it was a convenient base which kept her close to court. Anne had been promised that she would be able to come to court when she pleased. It soon became clear, however, that her visits were to be limited while Catherine settled into her position as queen. This was not Anne's choice and she readily accepted an invitation to court at New Year.

Anne arrived at Hampton Court on 3 January with a New Year's present for Henry of two fine horses decked out in mauve velvet. Upon her arrival,

Anne was taken for her first meeting with Catherine Howard as queen. Catherine was in a state of nerves about how to receive her predecessor and she kept Anne waiting while she discussed the correct etiquette for a current queen meeting an ex-queen with Henry's lord chancellor. Anne knew how important Catherine was to Henry and she had already determined to make friends with her rival. When Catherine finally entered, Anne threw herself to the ground at her feet with 'as much reverence and punctilious ceremony as if she herself were the most insignificant damsel about court, all the time addressing the queen on her knees'. Catherine had not been expecting this and she pleaded with Anne to get up but Anne refused, intent on showing Catherine that she fully accepted her as queen.

While Anne was still on her knees, Henry entered the room and made a low bow to his former wife before embracing and kissing her. For all three, the first meeting had been perfect and they sat down to dinner. Anne's attitude amazed onlookers and Eustace Chapuys, the Imperial ambassador, commented that she looked 'as unconcerned as if there had been nothing between them'. Anne had also, by that time, become fluent in English and, as the three talked after dinner, Anne and Catherine came to find that they had much in common and liked each other. When Henry retired to his own apartments, the two queens continued to sit talking, before dancing together happily. Dinner the next day was another success and, as the pair danced together, Henry sent Catherine a present of a ring and two small dogs. Catherine had grown so fond of Anne that she immediately made a gift of these to her predecessor, much to Anne's delight. The king also gave Anne a present of an annual rent of 1,000 ducats during the visit and, after a stay of two nights, Anne returned to Richmond, pleased with the way the visit had gone.

For her own self-preservation, Anne was determined to show the world that she was content with all that had happened to her. As early as August 1540 Marillac, the French ambassador, commented that Anne 'far from pretending to be married, she is as joyous as ever, and wears new dresses every day; which argues either prudent dissimulation or stupid forgetfulness of what should so closely touch her heart'. Anne's happy abandon was carefully constructed as a means of ensuring her survival and she threw even Harst into confusion with her apparent lack of concern over all that had happened. Anne knew that she had had little option but to publicly agree to the divorce and so she did so. That did not mean that she had to agree to it in private but the money she received, which she spent on luxuries such as clothes, was a consolation. Marillac commented that Anne, 'far from appearing disconsolate, is unusually joyous and takes all the recreation she can in diversity of dress and pastime'.

Anne's dissimulation was necessary as a means of survival but she was not the only person in England to believe that she was truly Henry's wife. By October 1540 there were dangerous rumours flying around court that Henry intended to discard Catherine and take Anne back as his wife. Anne would have welcomed this but she knew there was little prospect of it with Catherine in such high favour. That same month Henry's ambassador in Brussels also reported that a kinsman of Anne's had publicly said that he wished to see Anne reinstated as queen, and 'trusted to see the day that the king would repent of her repudiation'. Even Anne's visit to court, in which the king made such a show of Catherine as queen, raised rumours that Henry would take his former wife back with Marillac commenting that 'the king would rather have two [wives] than leave the present one'.

Even Catherine became concerned about these rumours. According to Chapuys, writing in May 1541:

I hear from a good source that this queen being some days ago rather sad and thoughtful, and the king wishing to know the cause, she declared to him that it was all owing to some rumour or other afloat that he (the king) was about to take back Anne de Cleves as his wife. To which the king replied that she was wrong to believe such things [of him] or attach faith to reports of the kind; even if he had to marry again, he would never retake Mme. de Cleves.

While Henry's answer ruled out a return for Anne, it is unlikely to have put Catherine at ease, particularly his reference to possibly taking a further wife in future. In spite of this, there was no sign that Henry intended to abandon Catherine and, in March 1541, at her first coming to London by water, he organized a grand pageant for her to rival that held for Anne the year before. It was notable that for Catherine's pageant, unlike Anne's, the king travelled in the same barge as his wife.

Anne and Catherine became friendly during Anne's visit to court, but there is no evidence that Anne returned to court during Catherine's time as queen and, instead, she made the most of her independence, going on a progress in the early months of 1541. Anne remained on Henry's mind and, in June 1541, when he was informed by Chapuys of Francis of Lorraine's marriage to Christina of Denmark, the king did his best to scupper the alliance, arguing: 'I hold that Anne de Cleves is the real and legitimate wife of the said marquis [Francis], for I myself have never seen or heard of any deed or authentic documents breaking through their mutual marriage engagement that being the chief reason and cause of my separation from her.' No one else considered Anne to be the wife of Francis of Lorraine and certainly not Anne or Francis themselves.

Henry was still besotted with his young wife when the couple went on progress together to York over the summer and autumn of 1541. Clouds were already gathering over their marriage while they were away however and, soon after the court returned to London, Archbishop Cranmer was approached by John Lascelles, a fanatical religious reformer, who informed him that his sister, Mary Hall, who had lived in the same household in which Catherine was raised, had told him that the queen was not as chaste as she had previously appeared.

On 2 November, Cranmer, concerned by the information that he had been given, passed a note to the king setting out what he had been told. Henry's first reaction was disbelief but, in order to clear his wife from such slander, he ordered that an investigation should be carried out. In spite of considerable pressure from Henry's commissioners, both Lascelles and his sister maintained their story. According to Lascelles:

Being with his said sister, chanced to fall in communication with her of the queen, wherein he advised her (because she was the queen's old acquaintance) to sue to be her woman; whereunto the sister answer'd, that she would not do so: but she was very sorry for the queen; 'Why,' quoth Lossels? 'Marry,' quoth she, 'for she is light both in living and condition.' 'How so,' quoth Lossels? 'Marry,' quoth she, 'there is one Francis Derrham, who was a servant also in my Lady of Norfolk's house, which hath lien in bed with her in his doublet and hose between the sheets an hundred nights. And there hath been such puffing and blowing between them, that once in the house a maid which lay in the house with her, said to me, 'she would lie no longer with her, because she knew not what matrimony meant.' And further she said unto him, that one Mannock, sometimes also servant to the said dutchess, knew a privy mark of her body.

Catherine had been raised in the household of her step-grandmother, the Dowager Duchess of Norfolk, and it was soon discovered that the Duchess had not kept the girls under her care as strictly as she might have done. Both Henry Mannox, Catherine's former music tutor, and Francis Dereham, a retainer in the Duchess's household, were also interrogated. Mannox confessed that he had felt Catherine's body in private although the pair had never had sexual intercourse. Dereham went further and admitted that he had both known Catherine carnally and that the couple had been secretly betrothed.

Henry was stunned by the news and 'his heart was so pierc'd with pensiveness, that long it was before his majesty could speak, and utter the sorrow of his heart'. His sorrow soon turned to fury at how he had been misled and he ordered Catherine's imprisonment and interrogation. After close interrogation, Catherine confessed to what Mannox and Dereham had said, although she always refused to admit a betrothal between Dereham and herself. By the time this confession reached the king it was already woefully inadequate and worse news about Catherine's conduct had been uncovered.

Catherine had apparently been in love with a young kinsman of hers, Thomas Culpeper, before her marriage to the king and she saw no reason for their relationship to cease upon her marriage. Shortly after she became queen, Culpeper wrote Catherine a letter, passing it to her secretly while they were dancing. Catherine wrote her only surviving letter to Culpepper and it is clear that she felt for him deeply, writing that 'I never longed so much for [a] thing as I do to see you and to speak with you'. With the help of Catherine's kinswoman, Lady Rochford, the couple met secretly in the queen's bedchamber both in London and while the court was on progress, with Catherine suspiciously ordering her ladies not to enter her bedchamber unless she called them. While Catherine and Culpeper always denied adultery, the evidence against them was damning and Catherine was sent as prisoner to Syon Abbey. Dereham and Culpeper were executed shortly before Christmas.

While the interrogations were still being carried out, Henry received word of another scandal, this time involving Anne. By late 1541, rumours were circulating that Anne had conceived a child by the king during her visit to court at New Year and that she had given birth to a son that summer. Henry, who knew full well that he was not the father of Anne's child, ordered a full investigation. He ranted to the council that, if it were proved to be correct he 'imputeth a great default in her officers, for not advising his highness thereof'. The council immediately sent for one of Anne's attendants, Lady Wingfield, to examine her. Another of Anne's ladies, Jane Rattsay, was also examined before the council was able to confirm that there was no truth in the rumours. Anne was completed exonerated but she was furious and this was yet further evidence that her conduct and household were under observation. At the same time as the examination into Anne's alleged child was being carried out, her lady, Jane Rattsay, was also examined by the Council for declaring of Catherine's fall 'what if God worketh this work to make the lady Anne of Cleves queen again?' Unbeknown to the king and council, Anne entirely shared these sentiments.

Although Anne had developed something of a friendship with Catherine she was not sorry for the fall of the woman who had supplanted her, rejoicing when she heard of Catherine's disgrace. Anne expected to be quickly reinstated as queen, even returning to Richmond so that she could be closer to the king. Anne's brother was also hopeful that a reconciliation could be arranged. On 29 November 1541, Olisleger made the first move, writing to the Earl of Southampton and asking him to favour Anne's affairs with the king. The following day Olisleger also wrote to Cranmer, asking him to assist in Anne's reinstatement. Harst was instructed to deliver the letters and they caused consternation with both their recipients. Southampton immediately forwarded his letter to the king, telling him that Harst had been instructed to 'seek to reconcile the Duke's sister with the king'. Cranmer also forwarded his letter to the king, cutting Harst short when he began to argue for Anne's marriage saying that he could discuss nothing without the king's consent. The reactions of Southampton and Cranmer were disappointing for Anne but both she and Harst remained convinced that her recall was imminent.

Harst also approached Marillac in order to obtain French assistance for Anne's reinstatement. Marillac, noting that Henry did not seem inclined to take Anne back, suggested that Harst wait to approach the king until after Catherine's fate had been determined. In answer to enquiries made by the Queen of Navarre, Marillac was able to assure her that Anne:

> Wants neither prudence nor patience. All her affairs could never make her utter a word by which one might suppose that she was discontented; nay, she has always said she wished nothing but what pleased the king her lord; thus showing an example of rare patience in dissembling passions common to everyone, which could only come of singular grace of God and a heart resolved to accept what could not be remedied. She has behaved, with her household, so wisely that those who visit her marvel at such great virtue, others who hear of it are loud in her praise, and all regret her much more than they did the late Queen Katharine [of Aragon].

Marillac concluded that Anne greatly desired remarriage. Henry however had no plans to return to Anne and he was deeply hurt by Catherine's betrayal. According to Marillac, 'he seems very old and grey since the mishap of this last queen, and will not hear of taking another, although he is ordinarily in company of ladies, and his ministers beg and urge him to marry again'.

Catherine Howard languished at Syon Abbey over Christmas 1541 before being attainted for treason by parliament in the New Year. With the passing of this Act her fate was sealed and she was brought by water to the

Tower on 10 February 1542. In the evening of 12 February, Catherine was informed that she would die the next day and, in order to prepare herself, she asked for the block to be brought to her so that she could practise laying her head on it. Early the next morning the Council assembled at Tower Green and Catherine was brought out to meet her death. It appears that she was able to say little on the scaffold although one report does credit her with declaring that 'I die a queen, but I would rather die the wife of Culpeper'. She died a queen indeed for Henry had not divorced her before her death as he had done Anne Boleyn. Catherine laid her head on the block and, with one stroke of the axe, Henry was again left free to marry.

With Catherine's death, Anne continued to hope that the king would return to her and it was some time before she would finally, and cruelly, have her hopes dashed.

12

The King's Sister:
February 1542 – January 1547

With Catherine Howard's execution, Anne became the only woman with a claim to be queen in England. She still retained her hopes that she would be recalled as queen and she waited patiently for her summons to court in early 1542.

Unbeknown to Anne, she was much on the king's mind early in 1542. In January, word reached Henry of a book that had been published in France, the author of which was apparently Anne. The book was known as the *Remonstrance of Anne of Cleves* and in it the author claimed that Anne was reduced to tears and so overwhelmed with sorrow at the end of her marriage that she was contemplating suicide. According to the *Remonstrance*:

> If tears and grief could remedy her misfortunes, she would not fail to employ them for the recovery of the goodwill which he ought to bear to her, seeing that she is a helpless stranger, who has left her native land, and the parents who so delicately nourished her, and the servants who loved and honoured her and who still regret her departure. But since she knows that great kings have always those beside them who represent their every wish as lawful, she has no hope except in his own goodness and equity; his own knowledge and sound judgment are her best defence, and if these fail, the eloquence of the greatest orator in the world would only render her very blameable in pretending to speak against what he might please to do.

In the book 'Anne' claimed that she would not dispute the legality of the divorce as Henry was 'one whom she only desires to honour and serve'.

The author also claimed that Anne was in love with Henry, stating of their marriage that 'its validity depends upon the mutual consent of the parties, stamped with the approval of the church; and this consent the king cannot deny that he gave. Is she now, in return for her plighted troth, to be robbed of honour and covered with shame'. The book finished with 'Anne' claiming that 'the law forbids her doing violence to herself, to send her soul back to heaven whence it came; yet she cannot live in the world without dying daily in deaths far more cruel than words can describe'. The book caused a sensation across Europe and Henry was furious.

While the *Remonstrance* was written as though it had been composed by Anne, it was clear to Henry and his council that she had nothing to do with it. It was still an embarrassment as the book was widely believed to represent the pitiable state of Henry's wronged queen. Henry's ambassador to France, Paget, obtained a copy in January and immediately sent it to Henry. Henry ordered Paget to approach Francis and request that he suppress the book. Paget did as he was ordered, complaining to the French king that the book was both slanderous and touched Henry's honour. Francis, interested, asked: 'What book is it? Who made it? Is it printed?' Paget replied: 'A very foolish book, sir.' Francis agreed to suppress the printing before adding that the book was folly 'especially now at this time; for men's affections do alter, and the lady Anne is yet of age to bear children, and albeit the wind hath been contrary it may fortune to turn'. Paget was discomfited by Francis's suggestion that Henry should take Anne back, merely replying that he knew nothing of the matter but that, in the divorce, Henry had 'acted with God's law, man's law, reason and honesty'. Henry's investigations found that the book was written by John of Luxembourg, a younger son of the Count of Brienne and a man who had no connection with Anne.

Anne continued to hope that Henry would take her back throughout the early months of 1542. The signs that she received from Henry seemed promising to her and, in March 1542, when she fell ill with a fever at Richmond, he sent servants to her to enquire after her health and to put his own doctors at her service. She received little other show of interest from Henry however and, during the early months of 1542, he showed no sign that he was looking to take a new queen at all, let alone taking back Anne. Anne also quickly became aware of why Francis had been so interested in seeing her reinstated as queen as, in the middle of 1542, the political situation in Europe exploded with direct consequences for her family in Cleves.

While Henry had assured William following the divorce that his friendship with Cleves remained unchanged, it was understood by everyone that Henry no longer considered himself bound to the terms of the marriage treaty. By the time of the divorce William was already looking around for other allies and, as early as 1540, there were rumours that he would marry Jeanne d'Albret, daughter of the King and Queen of Navarre and Francis's niece. With the breakdown in relations between Francis and Charles, William naturally gravitated towards Francis as an ally in his dispute with the emperor. As a sign of the alliance William travelled to France in 1541 where he married Jeanne d'Albret although, given the bride's youth, he left her in France when he returned to Cleves shortly afterwards.

Early in 1542 Charles travelled to Castile leaving the Low Countries under the governance of his sister, Mary of Hungary. This provided Francis and William with the opportunity they needed and on 12 July 1542 they declared war on Charles V, launching separate attacks on the Low Countries. The progress of the war went, at first, entirely in Francis and William's favour and, on 10 August 1542 Chapuys reported that Francis's son, the Duke of Orleans, was laying siege to Danvilliers. He continued that:

About the same time Mr de Longueval and Martin Van Rossem [William's commander], with 15,000 infantry, Germans (as is said) and from the duchies of Cleves and Ghelders, and upwards of 2,500 cavalry, penetrated into Brabant on the 15th. After some days spent in the neighbourhood of Bar-le-duc, sacking, destroying, and setting fire to the houses and fields of the poor peasantry, and carrying away what they could, they got possession of Hocstrate, and after that, on the 28th, encamped in sight of Antwerp, hoping no doubt, that being in secret intelligence with innumerable people from

Cleves and Ghelders, who had taken refuge inside, they might easily make themselves masters of that city.

The threat to Antwerp was a serious one and, as the chief city of the Low Countries, calculated to infuriate the Emperor. The siege of Antwerp was raised shortly afterwards but the danger to the city caused great anxiety in England and it was noted by Marillac, in his despatch to Francis on 1 August, that the fall of the city would cause great loss to the English merchants there. The chief men of London petitioned Henry to intervene in support of the city but he refused, replying that 'they had had warning that war was coming there, and leisure to put their goods in safety'. Henry was equally in no hurry to intervene on the side of Francis and William, in spite of the French king's invitation for him to join his great league against the Emperor.

The war went initially in favour of Francis and William but they soon lost momentum. Francis took Luxembourg quickly but it was soon recaptured and, in February 1542, Henry finally took decisive action as to which side he was on, concluding a secret pact with Charles to invade France within two years. By October 1542 the English ambassador to Mary of Hungary was also reporting that the Duke of Orleans 'had lost in eight days what cost him three months to take'. A further blow touched William more personally when the Burgundians intercepted 50,000 crowns which had been sent to him by Francis in order to support his war against Charles, leaving him in financial difficulties. In April 1543, the Emperor published his manifesto against the Duke of Cleves stating that William had 'usurped' Guelders and had 'carried on war against him [Charles], his natural lord and sovereign'. He continued, furiously, that 'the duke of Cleves has not only allied himself with the enemies of the Holy Empire and Christian republic, but has also so accustomed himself and his minsters to the manners and ways of those enemies, that he cannot speak one word of truth'. Charles was outraged by William's refusal to submit to his will and, in the summer of 1543, he finally arrived personally in the Low Countries to take action against his rebellious vassal. Anne watched everything happening with alarm from England but she had even more pressing concerns during 1542 and 1543.

Henry's court watched him closely after the execution of Catherine Howard, looking for signs that he intended to remarry. In early February 1542, even before the execution of Catherine Howard, Chapuys commented that, until the queen's condemnation:

> The king had shown no alacrity or joy, not even when he first heard of his queen's misdemeanour, but since he was informed of the trial and subsequent condemnation on the 29th he has considerably changed, for on the night of that day he gave a grand supper, and invited to it several ladies and gentlemen of his court. There were no less than 26 at his table including the gentlemen, and at another table close by 35. The lady for whom he showed the greater predilection on the occasion was no other than the sister of Monsieur Coban [Cobham] the same lady whom Master Huyet [Wyatt] did some time ago repudiate on a charge of adultery. She is a pretty young creature and has sense enough to do as the others have done should she consider it worth her while. It is also rumoured that the king has taken a fancy for the daughter of Madame Albart, the niece of the grand esquire Master Brown, and likewise for a daughter by the first marriage of the wife of Monsieur de Lyt [Lisle].

Henry decided against marrying any of these ladies, leaving Anne to continue to hope that he might turn back to her. She spent her time during 1542 and 1543 staying close to court and enjoying her own interests and pursuits. Anne visited the court in March 1543 spending three days there, although according to Chapuys she was ignored, with Henry only bothering to see her once. She had already been disappointed in her treatment earlier in the year and, in January, Chapuys commented that the ambassador of Cleves had been at court more than usual but that Anne, who was staying nearby at Richmond, was not summoned, in spite of her best efforts to secure an invitation. During this period Anne developed a close attachment to her former stepdaughter, Mary, who was only a year younger than her, and in June 1543 she welcomed the princess to Richmond for a visit. Mary enjoyed her stay and made a number of payments to Anne's servants and officers as a sign of her gratitude. The friendship continued to develop over the next few years and, in June 1544, Anne made Mary a present of some Spanish silk.

Mary had to return to court soon after her visit to Anne in order to attend an event to which Anne was most certainly not invited. On 12 July 1543, after over a year without a wife, Henry finally chose to marry again, his choice falling on a widow, Catherine Parr. Henry invited his two daughters, as well as his niece Lady Margaret Douglas, and most of his council to the wedding. After over a year without a queen everyone assembled was glad at the change in the king and when, during the ceremony, the witnesses were asked if they had any objections to the marriage, they applauded to signify their approval. Catherine Parr was thirty-one years old and had been widowed twice before her marriage to the king. Given her childlessness she was a surprising choice, but a popular one.

Just over two weeks after the marriage Henry came once again to Richmond to dine with Anne where he informed her of his sixth marriage. For Anne the news was devastating. While she had accepted the king's marriage to Catherine Howard with equanimity she had never considered that the king might choose to take a new wife. For Anne, it was Henry's infatuation with Catherine Howard that had led to the end of her marriage. Anne's reaction was one of shock but this quickly turned to anger. According to Chapuys writing on the day that Anne was officially informed of the marriage:

> I hear from an authentic quarter that the said dame [Anne] would rather lose everything in this world and return to her mother than remain longer in England, especially now that she is in despair and much afflicted in consequence of this late marriage of the king with a lady who, besides being inferior to her in beauty, gives no hope whatever of posterity to the king, for she had no children by her first two husbands.

In a further letter of the same day, Chapuys elaborated further, reporting that Anne would 'greatly prefer giving up everything that she has and living with her mother in Germany, to remaining any longer in England, treated as she is, and humiliated and hurt as she has lately been at the king marrying this last lady, who is by no means so handsome as she herself is'. For Anne, Henry's marriage was the final indignity heaped upon her and she was no longer prepared to tolerate her treatment, even if this meant the loss of her pension and the life she had built in England. Anne had never had any intention of being merely the king's sister; she wanted to be his wife. Anne was quickly to find that a return home had become impossible.

For Anne, there was bad news in June when word reached England that the armies of Charles and William had met in battle at Heneberge. The Prince of Orange, Charles's most loyal commander, led the Imperial forces, sending William's into retreat. William managed to regain some territory the following month but the Emperor's arrival in the Low Countries in late July was the beginning of the end for him. Charles was determined to crush William's opposition once and for all, bringing 18,000 footmen with him and 2,000 horsemen, as well as 4,000 Italian and the same number of Spanish footmen. This was a formidable force which William could in no way match. The Emperor also ordered that pressure be put on Henry to show his support for him, instructing Chapuys to speak to the king and ask him to expel William's ambassador. To Anne's relief, this was refused with the council informing him that 'they did not take him for ambassador, but as servant of the lady Anne of Cleves'. However, in the same dispatch Chapuys reported that both Anne and her ambassador wished to be away from England, but they were both trapped, with Anne forced to watch with mounting horror the situation in her homeland.

William had refused to believe that Charles would leave Spain in the summer of 1543 and the Emperor's arrival caught him entirely by surprise. He also found himself disappointed in his French allies: when he pleaded with the French king for aid, he received no response. In early August the Emperor entered William's lands with his forces. By 24 August Duren, the principal town of Juliers, was under siege and it fell within days. Charles was determined to make an example of the town, firing over 300 rounds of shot in the assault before burning the town and slaying many of the inhabitants. At the same time the Prince of Orange marched almost unopposed through Juliers, taking a castle in the highest part of the duchy. The loss of Duren was the end for William and, within days, the people of

Juliers brought the keys of the duchy to the Emperor. This was a disaster for William and a disaster for Anne in England and she listened closely to the news with despair.

Worse news was to follow for Anne. Her mother, Maria of Juliers, had been one of William's leading advisors, counselling him in his opposition to Charles. The loss of her own hereditary lands was too much for her and she died suddenly on 29 August, apparently of grief. This was terrible news for Anne who had hoped that she would one day be able to return to her homeland to live with her beloved mother again. William was also distracted with grief when he heard that his mother had 'departed this world raging in a manner out of her wits (as it is reported) for spite and anger of the loss of her country'. At Maria's funeral, William turned upon his council, blaming them for all that had befallen him and threatening them with death. He was restrained at the funeral but later attacked the French ambassador, accusing Francis of betrayal for failing to protect his lands.

With the loss of Juliers, William was entirely at the Emperor's mercy. Defeated and grieving he journeyed to meet Charles at Venlo on 7 September 1543 in order to sue for peace. Dressed in deepest mourning, William rode into the Emperor's camp and, kneeling before Charles:

> Owned and acknowledged that led away by juvenile passion and deceived by the counsels and persuasions of others, he had grievously offended his Imperial Majesty to pardon him his fault, and restore him to his favour. Upon which the Emperor, using clemency towards him, and with a view to prevent the continuation of a war which had so much afflicted, and might hereafter afflict, his own subjects in the duchy of Ghelders and county of Zutphen, accepted the Duke's submission and appointed some of his own councillors and ministers to treat with him of the terms of the peace.

William's complete submission was a requirement of the peace and Anne's brother was willing to entirely abase himself before Charles. As a result of this, he did not, in fact, fare too poorly in the peace and, while he was forced to hand over both Guelders and the other disputed territory,

Zutphen, Charles agreed to pass Juliers and William's other hereditary territories back to him. William also promised to ally himself with the Emperor, abandoning his alliance with Francis.

At Venlo William's marital status was a major source of discussion and it was agreed that he would divorce his French bride in order to marry one of the daughters of the King of the Romans. William was eager to show his new-found loyalty to Charles and, within days of their meeting at Venlo, Charles set out to march against the French, taking William's army with him. The war dragged on until the following year when Charles and Francis finally made peace. The terms of the peace treaty with France ensured that Jeanne d'Albret, William's wife, consented to a divorce. This was no great hardship to Jeanne who had never wanted to marry William and had always refused to live with her husband. William had already arranged a marriage to the Emperor's niece, Maria of Austria. The marriage was intended to bring William firmly into the Imperial party and Anne heartily approved of the match, sending her brother an extravagant gift of two horses and two braces of greyhounds as a wedding present.

For Anne, the years of William's war with the emperor were a time of worry. The political situation in her homeland remained bleak even after Charles's truce with France and, having brought one war to an end, Charles was finally able to move against the Schmalkaldic League. Anne's sympathies lay with her sister and brother-in-law in Saxony and she watched with despair as the League, which had played such an important part in her destiny, was destroyed in April 1547 and John Frederick captured by the Emperor. With the death of her mother, the loss of Guelders and the devastation of Juliers, it was yet another reminder to Anne that the home that she remembered no longer existed and that she would be forced to remain in England.

In spite of this, once it had become clear that the king had no plans to remarry her, she was at least able to settle back into her comfortable existence as a member of the royal family. In 1543 Anne's kinsman, Albert, Duke of Prussia, sent her a gift of a white osprey. In 1546, having put her differences with Catherine Parr behind her, Anne was also able to re-establish herself as a regular visitor to the court. In March it was recorded that she had already been for some time at court and she was notably well treated. In May it was also reported that Anne 'goes and comes to the court at her pleasure' and that she had an 'honest dowry' to live upon. In that same month she was listed as in attendance on the queen along with both the king's daughters and all three of his nieces and she was very much in evidence at court at that time. Henry behaved so kindly to Anne during these visits that rumours quickly began to circulate that the two had rekindled their relationship and that Anne had already borne the king two children.

In spite of the rumours surrounding their relationship, Anne and Henry settled into a comfortable rhythm during 1546 and Anne was very much a member of the royal family with, for example, the king including her in the surveys he ordered of jewel, plate, households and lands belonging to himself, his wife, Anne and his three children. Anne was also present at the reception for the Admiral of France held in London in August 1546 and she took part in the grand ceremonies to mark the event alongside Henry's two daughters and his niece, Margaret Douglas. This was Anne's last recorded meeting with Henry and she may have been struck by just how elderly and ill he suddenly appeared. By 1546 Henry had been the most important person in Anne's life for nearly seven years but, by the end of the year, it was clear that he was dying.

The man that Anne always considered to be her husband died on 28 January 1547, shut away from both his current wife and his ex-wife. For Anne, the news was a great blow and, while she had never been in love with the king, following the divorce she had become fond of him. With his death Anne was at a loss as to what to do for the future and, from the grand position of 'the King's Sister', she found herself suddenly relegated to only that of the king's aunt.

13

Everything is so Costly Here:
January 1547 – July 1553

With Henry VIII's death, Anne found herself bereft of a patron. Henry had provided for Anne generously in an attempt to ensure her continued acceptance of the divorce, and to keep her in England and under his control. With his death it no longer mattered whether Anne claimed to be his wife or not and, to the council of the new king, the nine-year-old Edward VI, Anne of Cleves was an expensive irrelevance.

Although convocation had declared Anne free to remarry in 1540, she never contemplated making a second marriage during the lifetime of the king and, in reality, it is inconceivable that anyone in England would have dared to marry the king's ex-wife. Following Henry's death (and the earlier death of Francis of Lorraine) there was no longer any question about Anne's marital status. This was something not lost on both the new king and his council and they would have welcomed a second marriage for Anne as a means of bringing to an end her financial dependence on the crown.

There is no evidence that Anne ever considered a second marriage for herself and, given her disastrous first attempt at matrimony, this is not really surprising. Once again, unwittingly, however, she found herself with a love rival in Catherine Parr. Catherine left court soon after Henry's death as was expected of a royal widow in mourning. Even before she had married Henry, she had been in love with Thomas Seymour, the brother of Henry's third wife, Jane Seymour. Seymour immediately recommenced his suit of the queen and within weeks of the old king's death they had come to an understanding to marry. The couple were eager to marry as soon as possible, but they were aware of the difficulty of their position and the scandal it would cause and Seymour set out to approach the king to gain his consent. In the spring of 1547 Seymour persuaded one of Edward's attendants, John Fowler, to approach the king and ask him who he thought Seymour should marry. According to Fowler:

> That night, his highnes being alone, I said to his majesty, 'And please your grace, I marvell my lord admiral marieth not.' His highnes saying nothing to it, I said again, 'Could your grace be contented he shuld mary?' His grace said, ye, very well. Then I asked his majesty whom his grace woold he shuld mary? His highness said, My Lady Anne of Cleves, and so, pawsing a whyle, said after, Nay, nay, wot you what? I woold he maried my sister Mary, to turn her opinions. His highness went his ways, and said no more at that time.

Seymour never had any intention of marrying Anne of Cleves when he could marry the queen. At that time Anne was entirely unaware of the king's suggestion but it quickly became clear to her that she could not expect the same level of financial support in the new reign as she had in the old.

Although in 1540 Anne's divorce settlement had been more than generous, by 1547 she was beginning to find that her finances did not stretch far enough. The last years of Henry VIII's reign and the reigns of his children were characterized by high inflation. The inflation became most rapid during the middle of the sixteenth century and, after centuries of price stability, came as a terrible shock to everyone. By the 1550s agricultural prices were, on average, about two and half times those of forty years before and 95 per cent above those in the 1530s. This was a major change and had grave consequences for people on fixed annual incomes such as Anne. There were a number of causes for this. Certainly, Henry VIII's debasements of the coinage did not help and, in 1553, one contemporary bemoaned the fact that the English coins were known to be either minted using base metals or produced using a lower weight of fine metals than was required. The contemporary concluded that, as a result of this:

It must be therefore confessed for the causes aforesaid that therefore there is given for our coin now of any wares outward or inward, not after that name that our coin doth bear, but after the value of the metal that is in it (as in things bought beyond sea doth well appear) for as in ten shillings of our money now, there is but two oz. of silver which was before in twenty groats sterling so ye have but so much ware for your ten shillings now as you had for twenty sterling groats before.

For Anne, the reduction in the value of the English coins was a disaster.

Unbeknown to her, she had been effectively shielded from the devaluation of her pension in the last years of Henry's reign by the generosity of the king himself. In September 1545, for example, Henry had paid over £22 to some of Anne's servants, to make up a shortfall in their wages. Two months later, Henry made further payments to members of Anne's household, including paying 100 shillings to her physician. In the days leading up to his death Henry granted an annuity to Anne's chamberlain, Sir John Guildford, ensuring that he was well rewarded for his service.

On 5 April 1547 Anne took the first steps in her battle for increased funds, sending a number of her officers to petition the council on her behalf, pointing out that her pension and other income left her with a yearly deficit in her accounts of over £120. This was a large deficit but the council, conscious that Anne had been promised her maintenance by Henry VIII, agreed to her request, confirming all grants made to her until the new king reached the age of eighteen. This was a victory for Anne, but it was a hollow one because on the same day the council also set out some of the changes that were intended towards her status and wealth during the reign of the new king.

While the council were considering Anne's pension and other incomes on 5 April 1547, they also resolved that she should be made to 'take the comodite of her house of Penthurste, deare and wodde within the park there, leaving in the lien thereof the comodite of Blechinglie, where it was alleged that she had the like graunte of thowse, deare and wodde'. Bletchingley was the second palace granted to Anne at the time of her divorce and, while she undoubtedly spent less time there than at Richmond, she was fond of the palace and had made it one of her homes. Anne was not the only person fond of the palace: Sir Thomas Cawarden, a member of Anne's household, made his interest in the palace clear. In December 1546 Henry VIII, in recognition of Cawarden's service as a member of his Privy Chamber, had granted him the reversion to Bletchingley, to be enjoyed after Anne's death.

Cawarden was not content only with the reversion to Bletchingley and, as a supporter of the religious reform, he became increasingly prominent in the reign of the Protestant Edward VI, enjoying the position of Master of the Revels which brought him into close contact with the king. Once Edward had become king he wasted no time in attempting to wrest Bletchingley from Anne and, within months of the king coming to the throne, the council wrote to Anne informing her of what had been decided in relation to Bletchingley:

> Madam, after due commendacions, wheras amonges other things declard here oon your behalf by Sir John Guldford, knight, your Graces chamberlain, the same hath required an estate to be made unto you of the use of the kinges Majesties house at Penshurst, the game and wood within the parke, in like mannour and forme as ye have presently at Blechinglegh, likeas we consydre that the commoditie of the sayd house of Penshurst shallbe mete for your purpose in respect of the nerenes of the same to Heyvour, and that forbearing nowe the commoditie of the house, game and woodes at Bleachinglegh aforsayd, the rest of your revenues there shall stande you in no other stede and pleasor but for the certeyn rent of the same; we have thought good, in respect of the determinacion which we know to have been in the kinges majestie, our late sovereign lorde decessed, to plante Sir Thomas Cawarden, knight, Gentleman of his Hieghnes Pryvie Chambre, in those parties when your Grace shuld receive other recompence, by theis to require your Grace to be content to make surrender unto him of all your title and interest at Bleachinglegh for the mannour and thappurtenances, payeng the yerely rent of xxxiiij poundes xv shillings and twoo pennes sterling, with such assuraunce to be made unto him of the same as by the lerned counsaill of your Grace and him shalbe thought convenient, wherein your Grace shall

for the tyme have such a tenante as will see your revenue assuredlye and honestly answered, and besides satisfie the determinacion of our sayd late Sovereign Lorde towards him, which we doubt not your Grace will please to tender the rather upon this our informacion of the same.

It was certainly Henry's intention that Cawarden should receive Bletchingley eventually, but he did not intend that it should be taken from Anne during her lifetime. Anne already made use of Hever Castle in Kent and had no interest in the nearby Penshurst, preferring to retain Bletchingley for her own use. She had no choice however and Cawarden was quickly ensconced as Anne's tenant at the palace. Cawarden also immediately set about making changes to the local church, something of which Anne, who remained a Catholic throughout her life, would not have approved. Cawarden's changes included pulling down the rood-loft in the church, white-washing the interior and defacing the altars.

Anne was angry with Cawarden for his actions in securing Bletchingley from her but she still relied on his services as a member of her household and paid him visits to Bletchingley and his London residence in Blackfriars. Anne's visit to Blackfriars was a lavish affair and Cawarden later petitioned the council for his expenses in providing for her. Even before her arrival Anne sent Cawarden a list of provisions she required. These included vast quantities of beer and wine for her household's consumption, as well as such exotic fare as ginger, cloves, pepper, raisons and prunes. Anne requested mutton and capons and great quantities of flour, again for her household's consumption. Other provisions necessary included wood for burning and candles and torches for the house.

If this was not enough, Anne and her household proved to be far from exemplary houseguests. According to Cawarden:

Over and besides, divers sondry fayer potts of pewter, by the seide Sir Thomas then bowght, provided, and paid for, to serve in the buttery for howshold, wherof he asketh no allowance for that, althowgh the most parte were spoyled, broken, and loste, the rest remayne in his howse and to his use; and over and besides brass, iron and latten potts, panes, kettles, skelletts, ladles, skimmers, peeles, dressing-knives, spitts, racks, fflesh-hookes, tubbes, baskets, trays, flaskets, and diverse other utensiles and properties ffurnished in theire places in the saide office, bowght, provided, and paid for by the seide Sir Thomas, to the valew of ixl vis viiid, partly then spoyld, broken, and loste, whereof he asketh no allowance for yt the rest remayne in his house to his use.

Anne's household left a trail of destruction, to Cawarden's alarm. Anne also indulged an interest in cooking while staying with Cawarden and, according to his report 'and over and besides sundry kindes of ffish, as carpes, pikes, tenches, and other ffresh ffishe, by him at the like request provided, and were privately drest in her seide [Grace's] laundres kittchin for the tryall of cookery'. Anne had little to occupy her time following the divorce and developed an interest in cooking, indulging in her hobby in private away from the busy main kitchen.

Anne soon discovered that Cawarden's appropriation of Bletchingley was not the worst of the council's interest in her property. She had been granted Richmond for life but she had spent next to nothing on the property in maintenance over her seven years of ownership, instead seeing this as the king's responsibility. This infuriated the council and it soon became clear that the king and his council desired its return. Anne held out against this pressure for some time, intent on retaining her home. By May 1548 she had already been forced to leave the palace but made one final personal plea to the council, arriving at court 'to speak to the Protector on certain complaints as to her treatment in many matters, and especially as regards the recompense for her house at Richmond, which has been taken away from her and prepared for the king'. Anne was given a favourable reply by the Protector, perhaps in an attempt to get her to leave court quietly, but the promises made were not kept and, on 3 June 1548, Anne finally surrendered the palace to the king. Edward immediately put in place a series of repairs to the dilapidated palace, spending £1,000 on emergency works there in the first year. The following year he was forced to pay a further £1,073, again demonstrating the dilapidated state that Anne had let her palace fall in to. The king was able to pay more reasonable sums on maintenance in subsequent years.

Bletchingley and Richmond were not the full extent of the new king's interest in Anne's property and, by 1552, pressure was brought to bear on her to relinquish her lands and manor at Bisham. Anne was notified of the required exchange in April 1552 but once again put up a fight, insisting that she was fairly recompensed for the loss. A letter of Anne's to Princess Mary written in January 1553 sets out many of the details of the exchange:

> It may please you to be advertised that it hath pleased the king's majesty to have in exchange my manor and lands of Bisham, in the county of Berkshire, granting me in recompense the house of Westropp [Westhorpe] in Suffolk, with the two parks and certain manors thereunto adjoining; notwithstanding, if it had been his highness' pleasure, I was well contented to have continued without exchange. After which grant, for mine own assurance in that behalf I have travailed, to my great cost and charge, almost this twelve months; it hath passed the king's majesty's bill, signed, and the privy seal, being now, as I am informed, stayed at the great seal, for that you, madam, be minded to have the same, not knowing, as I suppose, of the said grant. I have also received at this Michaelmas last passed, part of the rent of the aforesaid manors. Considering the premises, and for the amity which hath always passed between us (of which I most heartily desire the continuance), that it may please you therefore to ascertain me by your letters or otherwise, as it shall stand with your pleasure.

The last thing Anne wanted was to come into conflict with Mary who was both her friend and the heir to the throne but she wanted adequate compensation and Westhorpe was an acceptable exchange. Throughout Edward's reign Anne found her property under attack and, in 1552, attempts were made to force her to exchange her lands in Kent.

Even a change of government in England had little effect on the difficulty of Anne's position. The new king's uncle, Edward Seymour, had been appointed as Lord Protector shortly after his nephew came to the throne and created himself the Duke of Somerset. This appointment was not universally popular and certain members of Edward VI's council were dissatisfied in Somerset's rule, culminating in his arrest in October 1549 and the forced surrender of his Protectorship early the next year. Somerset was able to return as a member of the Council the following year but the king's new chief minister John Dudley, Duke of Northumberland, was working against him. In October 1551 Somerset was arrested for treason and executed on 22 January 1552. The fall of Somerset had little appreciable impact on Anne's treatment and it is clear from the letter that she wrote to her brother at the time of Somerset's fall that her own predicament was much more clearly on her mind. According to Anne 'God knows what will happen next; and everything is so costly here in this country that I don't know how I can run my house'.

Anne's financial troubles continued to worsen throughout Edward's reign and she was anxious to return home to Cleves, providing that she could find some way to keep her pension. From March 1547 William had regularly sent ambassadors to England to speak on Anne's behalf about her finances and, in July 1551 one ambassador, Dr Cruser, achieved something of a breakthrough. According to one report:

> after several petitions to the English Council about the allowance and household of my lady (Anne), the Duke's sister, the councillors came to an agreement, as the ambassador himself told me. According to his account, they have behaved reasonably enough; and it seems the archbishop of Canterbury shewed the said lady favour.

Anne was hopeful about the council's promise but these hopes were soon dashed. In August 1552 she was again forced to petition the council for funds and received the unfavourable response that 'his Highnes is presently in Progresse and resolved not to be trobled with payments until his returne, the same cannot be satisfied until his Majesties coming to London'. This was not the answer Anne wanted and while, the following April, payments were made to her officers by the council, they were not enough to satisfy her requirements as she had been in debt since June 1550.

Throughout Edward's reign Anne found it impossible to run her household and live as she was accustomed to and she longed to return to

Cleves. She retained a keen interest in the affairs of her homeland and, in November 1547 petitioned the king for him to request the release of John Frederick from the Emperor's captivity. Anne's approach was co-ordinated with a plea sent by Sybylla and her children and Edward did instruct his ambassador to speak for the captured Elector, but he was unable to persuade Charles to take action. For Anne it was a relief when, on 23 July 1552 the council wrote to her to inform her of John Frederick's release. This personal notification was a kind action and Anne was grateful but the news did nothing to lessen her feelings of homesickness.

For Anne, the years of Edward's reign were years of troubles and financial worries. While she was sometimes at court during the reign, the loss of Richmond meant that she no longer had a permanent base close to the court and she became increasingly isolated. Circumstances changed suddenly however and, on 6 July 1553 the fifteen-year-old king died, leading once again to a change in Anne's fortunes.

14

Favourable Treatment:
July 1553 – July 1554

The death of Edward VI was initially kept secret while the Duke of Northumberland prepared for the accession of his own daughter-in-law, Lady Jane Grey. Anne played no role in the brief reign of Queen Jane but, along with everyone else in England, she watched events anxiously. Princess Mary had always been Anne's friend and she supported her claim over the unknown Jane Grey. It was with satisfaction that Anne greeted news of the proclamation of Mary as queen in London on 19 July 1553.

Anne immediately found herself more in demand at court under Mary than she had since the early days of her divorce from Henry VIII. She had been sidelined during Edward's reign and made to feel unwelcome at court, but Mary was determined to obey the terms of Anne's divorce agreement and give her the status and respect she was due. The first sign of this change in treatment was in the preparations for Mary's coronation, which was set for the autumn of 1553.

On 28 September, Mary took her barge, accompanied by most of the nobility in England, to the Tower. It is probable that Anne was among the ladies dressed in their finery as they sailed down the Thames. As the procession sailed, it was met by the mayor and aldermen of London who came out in boats decorated with streamers and, as it landed, a great peal of guns was fired from the Tower. After dinner on 30 September, the entire court assembled and:

Proceeded from the Tower through the city of London towards the palace of Westminster. The streets were well gravelled and railed on one side from

Gracechurch [street] to the little conduit in Cheapside, that the horses should not slide on the pavement. Within the rails the crafts of London stood in order to the conduit where stood the aldermen. There was presented to the queen by the chamberlain of London in the name of the mayor, aldermen and whole city 1000 marks in gold, for which her highness gave thanks. On either side the windows and walls were garnished in tapestry, arras, cloth of gold and tissue, with cushions of the same, garnished with streamers and banners. In many places ordained goodly pageants and devices, and therein great melody and eloquent speeches of noble histories treating of the joyful coming of so noble and famous a queen.

The procession was intended to demonstrate Mary's power and her right to the crown as the legitimate heir to the Tudor dynasty. Mary, wearing an elaborate dress of blue velvet trimmed with ermine, sat in a chariot draped in fine tissue and drawn by six horses trapped with red velvet. On her head she wore a veil of tinsel set with pearls and stones and, on top of this, she wore a circlet of gold, so heavy and set with stones that she had to hold up her head with her hands as the chariot passed through the streets. A canopy was held over Mary's chariot and in front of her rode a procession of knights and gentlemen, as well as judges, ambassadors and other dignitaries. Mary's council also rode in front of her with the Earl of Oxford bearing the sword of state. Crowds thronged the streets on either side, hoping to get a glimpse of the first woman in England to be crowned as queen in her own right.

Anne was well aware that this was the first time a queen had been crowned since 1533 and the coronation of the ill-fated Anne Boleyn. For Anne of Cleves, the ceremony may have been bitter-sweet as she remembered the plans that had been made for her own coronation. Anne was given a prominent place in Mary's coronation procession. According to the anonymous *Chronicle of Queen Jane and Two Years of Queen Mary*, after Mary's chariot:

Came another chariot having canapie all of one-covereng, with cloth of silver all whit, and vi horses betrapped with the same, bearing the said charyat;

and therin sat at the ende, with hir face forwarde, the lady Elizabeth; and at the other ende, with her back forwarde, the lady Anne of Cleves. Then cam theyre sondry gentyllwomen rydyng on horses traped in red velvet, after that charyet, and their gownes and kertelles of red velvet likewise.

Anne was glad of the confirmation of her status by her place in the first chariot after the queen, riding with the heir to the throne. She and Elizabeth wore matching dresses of crimson velvet. Anne's presence did cause some curiosity and one observer remarked that Anne 'once upon a time had hardly been fully married to King Henry when she was nevertheless excluded from the royal bed, for what reason I do not know'.

Facing backwards in her chariot, Anne could see the end of the procession as it wove its way through the streets. She watched avidly whenever the procession stopped to view pageants at various places along the route. In one, a child sitting in a chair was lifted by two men and saluted the queen as she passed. Another, more elaborate, pageant was staged at the end of Gracechurch Street. The pageant was made up of pictures and at its top stood the model of an angel, clothed in green and holding a trumpet. When a trumpeter, who stood concealed within the model, blew his own instrument, the pageant angel raised his trumpet to give the appearance that he played the music himself 'to the marvaling of many ignorant persons'. As the procession moved on, Anne saw children at Cornhill dressed as Grace and Virtue singing verses to Mary. Streamers were hung from the steeple of St Paul's with the arms of the city of London fluttering in the wind. For Anne, after her years of living quietly, it was a magnificent spectacle and she congratulated the queen as the procession arrived at Westminster Palace.

Mary's coronation was arranged for the next day and, on the morning of 1 October, she again set out in procession to Westminster Abbey. There is no record of Anne attending the ceremony in the Abbey although she may have been there. Both Anne and Elizabeth attended the coronation banquet that followed and the pair sat at the same table as Mary as everyone dined in candlelight in Westminster Hall. Following the meal Mary took to her barge and Anne is likely to have been in the procession again. For Anne, her prominent place was a sign that she would now enjoy royal favour. Mary's coronation was to be Anne's last public appearance but her close relationship with the queen meant that she was able to make some forays into politics after years of obscurity.

One of Mary's first priorities on becoming queen was the restoration of traditional religion in England. She had never conformed to Protestantism during her brother's reign, instead remaining attached to the religion of her childhood. Anne had also been raised as a Catholic but the absence of any reference to her religion during Edward's reign suggests that she conformed to the reformed faith.

Mary's changes to religion happened quickly and by August the Spanish ambassador, Simon Renard, was able to report that:

> Last Sunday a solemn predication was held at St Paul's by a doctor who has long been associated with the Bishop of Winchester. Several members of the queen's council were present, and the yeomen of the guard, for the protection of the said preacher, who discoursed pertinently on the holy sacrament. The sermon was well received, without murmurs or interruptions. Mass is sung habitually at Court; not one mass only, but six or seven every day, and the Councillor's assist. My ladies of Cleves and Elizabeth have not been present yet. On Saint Bartholemew's Day mass was sung at St Paul's; matins and vespers are already being recited there in Latin.

The high altar was set up once again in St Paul's Cathedral and crucifixes and other features of Catholicism were replaced in churches across London. That Anne was particularly mentioned by the Spanish ambassador demonstrates her prominence at court during the early days of Mary's reign and her association with Elizabeth. There is no evidence that Anne ever really adopted Protestantism and she died a confirmed Catholic. Mary expected both her former stepmother and her half-sister to conform to her faith, just as she did the rest of her country. Anne was happy to do so and quickly began attending mass when it was clear that this was expected of her. By early September Mary had informed the Imperial ambassador that she intended to return England to obedience to the pope.

There had never been an effective queen regnant before Mary and no one in England or on the continent seriously believed that she would be able to rule alone. It was unheard of for a queen to remain unmarried and Anne, along with everyone else, expected the thirty-seven-year-old queen to rapidly marry and provide England with a king. As soon as Mary came to the throne candidates for her hand began to make themselves known. At least seven names were put forward: the King of Denmark, Prince of Piedmont, Archduke Ferdinand of Austria, Don Luis of Portugal, Prince Philip of Spain, Edward Courtenay, Earl of Devon and even Mary's cousin, Cardinal Pole. Most of these men were not serious candidates but rumours throughout the latter half of 1553 were rife about who the queen would marry.

Anne had her own ideas about who Mary should marry and, encouraged by the favour in which she found herself during the early months of the reign, she set about trying to ensure that the queen married to the best advantage of Cleves and, of course, of Anne herself. According to Simon Renard, in October 1553, Anne went to the queen and spoke directly to her about marriage:

> My lady of Cleves has spoken to the queen about a marriage with the Archduke (Ferdinand), and Paget has had letters from the ambassador sent to Hungary by the late Duke of Northumberland before the late King Edward's death, speaking of the same matter and saying that the king of the Romans is greatly desirous of seeing the marriage arranged.

The Archduke Ferdinand, who was the eldest son of Charles V's brother, the King of the Romans, was William of Cleves's brother-in-law. Anne considered him the perfect husband for the queen as the match would ensure that good relations with her homeland would be maintained. It seems likely that the Archduke himself would have requested Anne's support in the marriage and certainly William required his well-placed sister to speak in favour of such an advantageous marriage. Anne was flattered to find herself of such importance and she set about attempting to persuade her friend to marry her chosen candidate.

Anne was not the only person to speak for the Archduke. The King of the Romans sent an ambassador to Mary in November 1553. He arrived bearing letters from his master and was disconcerted when Mary refused to see him, claiming to be unwell. The king had previously sent ambassadors to his brother the Emperor, requesting his support in arranging the marriage for his son. Charles had sent no response to these letters, something which prompted the king's despatch of his own ambassador to England and, perhaps also, his determination to use Anne as an advocate for the Archduke. By November 1553, unbeknown to both Anne and the King of the Romans, Mary had already decided upon a husband and, in private, she told Renard that, while the king was 'doing her greater honour than she deserved by making such proposals, [he] [Renard] had made her fall in love with his Highness'. The man Mary had fallen in love with was the Emperor's son, Philip of Spain.

Charles V was eager for his son to marry Mary and he was not prepared to allow his nephew to be considered. He instructed Renard that, if the Archduke Ferdinand was suggested, he was to tell the queen that he was not a suitable husband for her. Since the divorce of her parents, Mary had relied on her cousin the Emperor for emotional support. In one of her earliest conversations with Renard following her accession, Mary confirmed that she had always viewed Charles as a father and that she would not marry without his consent. This was more than Charles had hoped and he wrote to his son to suggest the match. Philip, a serious-minded widower in his late twenties, was attracted by the prospect of another crown and, in November 1553, Mary received the proposal that she so desperately wanted and happily accepted.

Anne was disappointed at the failure of her plans for Mary's marriage and she was not the only person in England to be upset by the queen's choice. On 6 November Renard spoke to Stephen Gardiner, Mary's Lord Chancellor, in an attempt to gain his support for the Spanish marriage. Gardiner responded that he preferred an English marriage and that he felt 'it would be difficult to induce the people to consent to a foreigner'. The leading English candidate, Edward Courtenay, was never taken seriously by Mary and, having spent over half his life in the Tower as a consequence of his descent from Edward IV, he was reckless and hot-blooded and entirely unsuitable to be a king. Not everyone in England saw it that way however.

Following the announcement of the Spanish marriage, there were mutterings of discontent across the country. By the end of the year a group of noblemen had formed a conspiracy against the marriage, with the aim of putting Elizabeth, married to Edward Courtenay, on the throne. There were to be four strands to the rebellion, with a rising in Herefordshire led by Sir James Crofts, one in the south-west led by Sir Peter Carew and Courtenay, one in Leicestershire led by the Duke of Suffolk, the father of the imprisoned Lady Jane Grey, and the fourth in Kent to be led by Sir Thomas Wyatt. Courtenay proved to be the weakest link in the conspiracy and, on 21 January 1554, he confessed to his friend, Gardiner, what was planned. Gardiner immediately informed Mary but, while most of the rebellions never even began, by 21 January Wyatt was already in Kent.

On 25 January 1554, Wyatt rode into Maidstone market and issued a proclamation, stating that even the Catholics in England would 'gladly embrace his quarrel against the Strangers'. He set out his justification for the rebellion, stating that:

> Forasmuch as it is now spread abroad, and certainly pronounced by [Stephen Gardiner, Bishop of Winchester] the lord chancellor and others of the [Privy] Council, of the queen's determinate pleasure to marry with a stranger, & c. We therefore write unto you, because you be our friends, and because you be Englishmen, that you will join with us, as we will with you unto death, in this behalf; protesting unto you before God, that no earthly cause could move us unto this enterprise but this alone: wherein we seek no harm to the queen, but better counsel and councillors; which also we would have foreborne in all other matters, saving only in this. For herein hath the health and wealth of us all.

Wyatt claimed that the Spaniards were already at Dover and urged all loyal citizens to rise 'for the advancement of liberty and common wealth'.

His proclamation was well received by the people of Kent and, later that day Wyatt, accompanied by a growing force, marched to Rochester.

The queen immediately sent an army out to meet the rebels but there was little she could do to stop the spread of the rebellion and, still denying that he was a traitor, Wyatt moved on to Dartford, spending the night of 31 January there. When Mary sent men to Wyatt offering to negotiate with him he refused unless he was given custody of the queen and the Tower. With the rebels rapidly approaching, Mary took decisive action and went to the Guildhall where she made the speech of her life, rallying the people with her claim that the marriage was only arranged with the consent and advice of her council. Using an image that would later be used effectively by her half-sister, Mary also called her marriage to Philip her second marriage stating that:

> I am already married to the Common Weal and the faithful members of the same; the spousal ring whereof I have on my finger: which never hitherto was, nor hereafter shall be, left off. Protesting unto you nothing to be more acceptable to my heart, nor more answerable to my will, than your advancement in wealth and welfare, with the furtherance of God's glory.

Mary's speech was decisive and when, on 3 January, Wyatt marched upon Southwark, he found the gates of London Bridge locked and guarded against his approach.

For Wyatt, the failure of his troops to cross the bridge was a major setback and he waited for two days while he considered what to do. On 6 February he surprised everyone by marching his forces to Kingston where he crossed without incident. By the next morning, to the terror of everyone in London, he had reached Hyde Park. Once word of Wyatt's crossing reached Whitehall, panic seized the court and Mary was urged to flee with the cry of 'All is lost! Away! Away! A barge! A barge!' The queen helped to calm the situation, informing those assembled that they should 'fall to prayer! And I warrant you, we shall hear better news anon. For my lord will not deceive me, I know well. If he would, God will not: in whom my chief trust is, who will not deceive me'. Mary was correct when she said

that there would soon be better news and, once in London and beset by
the royal troops, Wyatt's courage finally failed and he was captured and
taken to the Tower.

With the capture of Wyatt and the defeat of his troops, the danger was
over. Mary ordered an investigation into the cause of the rebellion and
those behind it. Anne's whereabouts during the rebellion are not recorded
although she is known to have been at Hever Castle only a few months
later and may, perhaps, have been staying there during the danger. She
was not involved in the events of the rebellion, but she found herself under
suspicion, along with many of the people with whom she was associated.

According to Renard's despatch of 12 February 1554 Anne, along with
Elizabeth and Courtenay, was a focus of the government's anger:

> The Queen of England summoned me this morning and informed me that
> the Council had issued orders for Courtenay's arrest and imprisonment in
> the Tower, because Wyatt, without having been tortured, accused him and
> several others, such as Pickering and Poignz, of being of the conspiracy.
> Pickering escaped arrest by flight into France, where he is said to have joined
> Carew. A clerk of the queen's council, named Thomas (was also mentioned).
> The council has sent two of the queen's physicians to visit the Lady Elizabeth
> and find out whether she is still unwell or only pretending, and whom she
> has in her house; and if she is not ill the Admiral, Hastings and Cornwallis
> are to arrest and bring her to the Tower. The Queen, moreover, told me that
> the Lady (Anne) of Cleves was of the plot and intrigued with the Duke of
> Cleves to obtain help for Elizabeth: matters in which the king of France was
> the prime mover.

According to Renard, Mary informed him that she believed Anne to
be part of the conspiracy. This was partly due to her association with
Elizabeth and also the still close association with her brother that she had
demonstrated in her attempts to speak for the Archduke Ferdinand. On 8
February 1554, Renard had written that he expected the King of France to
make war on England in order to prevent the marriage and also 'because
he has promised the Duke of Cleves, at the lady Elizabeth's request,

thus to revenge himself for Henry VIII's repudiation of his sister, and in order to give the German princes an opportunity of turning their forces against your Majesty's dominions'. This idea was considered by Charles V himself on 18 February when he wrote to Renard that the King of France had made the promise to attack England to the Duke of Cleves, 'at his sister's request – she who was abandoned by the late King Henry – and by the intermediary of the lady Elizabeth'. To the Emperor, the Spanish ambassador and, it seems, the queen herself, Anne was as involved in Wyatt's rebellion as Princess Elizabeth and to many people the behaviour of another associate of both women, Sir Thomas Cawarden, would have seemed damning.

On 26 January, the day after Wyatt made his proclamation in Maidstone, Sir Thomas Cawarden was at Bletchingley when:

> Being in his house at Blechingly aforesaide in perfecte quyettnes, good order, obedience, and subjectelyke, between the howres of eight and ten in the morning, was by the lord William Hawade, James and John Skynner, arrested, apprehended, and caryed thens as a prisoner, and browghte before the lords of the Counsell in the Star Chamber, and there of Stephen Gardener, the late bishop of Winchester, then lorde chancellor, demaunded diverse and sondry questyons, which yor seide supplyaunte so aunswered as thereupon, dysmyssed, and sett at libertie.

Cawarden acquitted himself well in his interrogation and, on his release, was given letters ordering him to prepare himself and his servants and tenants at Bletchingley to march at an hour's notice against the rebels.

Cawarden's loyalty was still under question due to his known reformist sympathies and, the following day, he was ordered to meet Sir Thomas Saunders, the Sheriff of Surrey, one mile away from Bletchingley. Once there, Cawarden was informed that his munitions and armour were to be confiscated and that he was, once again, under arrest. Cawarden was taken up to London, protesting vigorously, where he was seen by Gardiner before being committed to house arrest at Blackfriars. The seizure of Cawarden's goods only helped to increase government suspicion against him as Bletchingley was found to contain such an extensive arsenal of weapons that seventeen cartloads were carried away from the house.

Whatever her personal feelings about Cawarden and his acquisition of Bletchingley, Anne remained associated with him and she continued to make use of Bletchingley on occasional visits. Princess Elizabeth had also had contact with Cawarden and a letter from her exists showing her favourable view of him. No involvement in Wyatt's rebellion was ever proved of either Elizabeth or Cawarden and it was the same for Anne. While both Cawarden and Elizabeth may at least have been aware of the rebellion, it seems unlikely that Anne was actively involved in anything so dangerous. She had, after all, only just come back into favour after her years in obscurity under Edward and she is unlikely to have wanted to jeopardize this, particularly when the queen was a personal friend of hers. In spite of Anne's lack of guilt, for Mary the relationship with her former stepmother was irreparably damaged and the coincidence of rumours of French and Clevian hostility, Anne's fondness for Elizabeth and her association with Cawarden were too much for Mary to forgive or forget.

Anne remained oblivious to the suspicion that she was under following Wyatt's rebellion and, on 3 April 1554, Dr Cruser arrived once again in England to act as ambassador and to 'congratulate the queen on her victory and marriage with his Highness on behalf of the Duke and Duchess of Cleves'. Cruser also 'thanked the queen for her favourable treatment of the Duke's sister', indicating that word of Mary's suspicions had not reached Cleves. Anne may have taken any coldness on Mary's part as evidence of the queen's preoccupation with her marriage preparations and, on 20 July 1554, Philip finally landed at Southampton, travelling to meet Mary at Winchester on 24 July. For Mary, the wedding on 25 July was the happiest day of her life and she touchingly requested that her wedding ring should be a plain band of gold 'because maydens were so married in olde tymes'. Celebrations throughout England were ordered by the queen and Anne, although she was not present at the ceremony, wrote to congratulate her friend:

After my humble commendations unto your majesty, with thanks for your loving favour showed to me in my last suit, and praying of your highness your loving continuance, it may please your highness to understand that I am informed of your grace's return to London again; and being desirous to do my duty to see your majesty and the king, if it may so stand with your highness' pleasure, and that I may know when and where I shall wait on your majesty and his. Wishing you both much joy and felicity, with increase of children to God's glory, and to the preservation of your prosperous estates, long to continue with honour in all godly virtue. From my poor house at Hever, the 4th of August.

Your highness' to command, Anne the daughter of Cleves.

There is no evidence that Anne was invited back to court and her return to prominence had ended almost as soon as it had begun. There was never an open breach between Anne and Mary, and they remained on cordial terms for the rest of Anne's life, but after Wyatt's rebellion the warm relationship that they had enjoyed had gone and Anne was forced back into her own household, finding herself at odds with the council once again.

15

Departed This Life at Chelsea: July 1554 – August 1557

Following her brief return to prominence during Mary's reign, Anne found herself forced back into her quiet and obscure life in England. Her final years were often frustrating and, in spite of her best efforts, she found herself less and less able to manage her own affairs without interference.

Anne's divorce settlement had been granted to her on the understanding that she remain in England. Henry VIII's reasoning for this had been in order to continue to keep Anne under his control and to prevent her from asserting the legitimacy of her marriage from abroad. This clause in the settlement had always rankled with Anne but she knew that she would be penniless if she returned home, and dependent on her brother's charity. By the early months of Mary's reign Anne had, however, come up with a solution that she hoped would change this position and, according to the Imperial ambassadors in October 1553:

> My lady (Anne) of Cleves is taking steps to get her marriage to the late King Henry VIII declared legitimate, so that she may enjoy the dowry, treatment and prerogatives of a Queen Dowager of England, and also continue to enjoy her dowry even if absent from England. We hear that the case will be adjourned till later, when more urgent and important affairs have been settled and decided.

Unlike Anne's divorce settlement, her marriage settlement had provided for her to return to Cleves as a wealthy widow. Anne had also considered herself Henry's rightful wife throughout the last years of his reign and, for her, a return to Cleves as a queen dowager would wipe away the stain of her rejection. She could be respected and independent in Cleves as a wealthy widow in a way that she could never be as a penniless divorcee. Her plan was doomed to failure, however, as the council never found time to consider her business, particularly after the withdrawal of the queen's favour in the spring of 1554.

For Anne, this was the end of her hopes and she finally admitted defeat. Her acceptance of her exile in England may have been helped by the news of another break with the past in April 1554 when Dr Cruser was sent to England to inform Anne of the deaths of both her brother-in-law, John Frederick of Saxony, and her sister, Sibylla. Anne's reaction to these deaths is not recorded, but they must have been a blow. There is no record that Anne had ever met John Frederick and she had not seen Sibylla since her childhood but, nonetheless, they were links to her homeland and, with their deaths, it became even more clear to Anne that there was no possibility that she would ever return home to Cleves.

With her difficulties at court and the final abandonment of her hopes of returning home, Anne retreated into her household. Even there, she often found that both Mary's council, and her brother, involved themselves in her affairs, to her chagrin. When she had first come to England, Anne had brought a young man called Florence de Diaceto with her from Cleves. Diaceto remained in England following her divorce and was in Anne's service at the time of Mary's accession. This length of service suggests that Anne was fond of the young man and she was angered when he was dismissed by the queen's council. Diaceto, realizing the trouble he was in, left England and travelled to Paris where he was spied upon by English agents who reported that 'it should seem he is here for no good intent'.

Diaceto was considered to be a troublemaker by the queen and her council. However, the young man had his own account of all that had happened, sending a claim to the queen in 1555 for sums due to him during his time in England. According to Diaceto, he had been sent to Denmark on the orders of Edward VI, near the end of that king's reign. While there he was forced to incur a high level of personal expense before being ordered to return upon Mary's accession. Diaceto unfortunately timed his return with Wyatt's rebellion and his bag, containing all his writings and a gold chain given to him by the King of Denmark, was seized by agents of the crown and not returned to him. To add insult to injury, Diaceto's pension, which he had been granted for coming over to England in Anne's train, was stopped, and pressure was put upon him to stay away from England for good. In his appeal, Diaceto continued pointing out his fifteen years of service and that, 'If her majesty should not reward me, I would be the only one of the foreigners to have devoted time and money to the service of this realm without recompense.' Anne bitterly resented any interference in her household and, whatever the truth of the dispute between Diaceto and the council, her sympathies were entirely with her countryman. The dismissal of Diaceto was not the only interference that Anne suffered in her household during the last years of her life.

In 1547, one of Anne's countrymen, Jasper Brockehouse, had been appointed to act as her cofferer. By 1552 Anne's expenses exceeded her income by nearly 1,000 pounds a year and Brockehouse set about attempting to reduce his mistress's expenses. This made him supremely unpopular with Anne's servants, particularly with her cousin, Count von Waldeck, who moved into Anne's household as a semi-permanent guest with eight servants of his own. Waldeck's expensive presence brought him into conflict with Brockehouse and when Waldeck returned to Cleves he was able to convince William of Brockehouse's untrustworthiness.

Brockehouse was not the only member of Anne's household to have earned the hatred of Count von Waldeck and, upon his return to Cleves, he persuaded William that Brockehouse, his wife and another servant, Otho Wyllik, ought to be dismissed from Anne's service. Anne was fond of Waldeck, but her sympathies in this matter were entirely with Brockehouse and her other servants and, when William broached the subject with her, she refused to dismiss them. Anne resented the interference into her household and the family of servants that she had built around her and she quickly became angry when she discovered that William intended to continue with his attempts to dismiss them. On 5 August 1556 William wrote personally to the queen asking that she assist him in the expulsion from England of the three. He complained particularly of Brockehouse's wife, Gertrude, lamenting that 'by her marvellous impostures and incantations' she seemed to have driven Anne mad. Waldeck's reports were behind this and Anne was by no stretch of the imagination mad. She was however furious with her brother and refused absolutely to listen, even with the added pressure of the queen's intervention.

William was not content with merely approaching Mary and he persisted in his efforts by petitioning the queen's husband, Philip of Spain. Philip was prepared to assist William and wrote to the Council in England asking them to intervene. They were able to reassure him that:

> Touching the request of the duke of Cleves for putting [Jasper]] Brockhuse, his wife, and one other from the service of Lady Anne of Cleves: the queen willing us to have special care of this, we have already begun to inform ourselves whereby, with your and the queen's honour and as little offence to Lady Anne as may be, this may be as the duke requires. We trust in a few days to make an end.

Philip took a personal interest in the matter, writing back to the council only three days later that 'what you report concerning the sister of the Duke of Cleves is pleasing. We desire that this is carried out by you, and reported to us as soon as possible'.

On 14 September 1556, the council ordered Jasper Brockehouse, Otho Wyllik, Stephen Vaughan and Thomas Chare to appear before them the following week. All four were members of Anne's household and the summons caused uproar in her usually quiet establishment. Anne was reluctant to let them go, but there was little she could do. On 17 September the men appeared before the council to receive their judgment. Brockehouse was given until 22 September to 'departe from the house and family of the lady Anne of Cleve, and come never after in any of the same lady's houses, or where she shall for the tyme make her abode, ne do entromedle or busye himself in thadministracion of the government of her howseholde or other her affaires as her servant or officer'. Brockehouse and his wife were also ordered to leave England before All Saints' Day and to return only 'at their uttermost perilles'. Otho Wyllick received the same judgment, being given only two weeks in which to depart from England. It was nearly two weeks before the council bothered to write to Anne directly to inform her of their decision.

Anne continued to find her independence thwarted in the early months of 1557 and, on 29 April 1557, Sir Thomas Cornwaleys wrote to Sir William Cecil complaining of what he saw as Anne's stubbornness in another forced exchange of property. The property that Anne was being urged to exchange was Westhorpe in Suffolk, a property that she had already acquired through an exchange and was anxious to retain. According to Cornwaleys 'she cannot be dissuaded from Westropp, unless recompensed with the house and park at Gulford'. Once again, Anne's household was blamed for her stubbornness and Cornwaleys reported that 'her Grace's disposition towards Westropp is increased by procurement of Mr Freston, cofferer'. It seems to have escaped everyone's notice that Anne might have had strong feelings about the property itself which the members of her household merely reported and, by early 1557, she was seen as a tiresome relic of the past by many in England in her attempts to maintain her household and stand up for her rights.

Anne had been in ill health for some time and, by the end of April 1557, she was a very sick woman. In the spring of that year she moved to Chelsea, a house that had been a favourite of one of her successors as Henry's wife, Catherine Parr. While there, Anne's health grew steadily worse and, by 12 July, she had taken to her bed, aware that she was dying. At the end of her life Anne was left alone with her household, who were her closest companions and she spent considerable time over her will which was drafted on 12 July. In her will, Anne declared that:

We, Anna, daughter of John, late duke of Cleves, and sister to the excellent prince William, now reigning duke of Cleves, Gulich (Juliers), and Barre, sick in body, but whole in mind and memory, thanks be to Almighty God, declare this to be our last Will and testament. 1st we give and bequeath our soul to the holy Trinity, and our body to be buried where it shall please God. 2dly, we most heartily pray our executors undernamed to be humble suitors for us, and in our name, to the queen's most excellent majesty, that our debts

may be truly contented and paid to every one of our creditors, and that they
will see the same justly answered for our discharge.

Anne's concern throughout her will was for her household and she
requested that the queen grant her the rents from her lands at Michaelmas
which, due to her interest in the land only being for the duration of her
life, would not be ordinarily payable to her. From these payments she
hoped that the expenses of her household would be met. She also begged
her executors:

> To be good lords and masters to all our poor servants, to whom we give and
> bequeath every one of them, being in our check-roll, as well to our officers
> as others, taking wages either from the queens highness or from us, from the
> current month of July, one whole year's wages, also as much black cloth, at
> 13s. 4d. per yard, as will make them each a gown and hood.

Anne left bequests of money to her ladies, including gifts of £20 and £100
respectively to Susan Boughton and Dorothy Curzon for their marriages.
Anne remembered to leave bequests for her laundress and also for a
Mother Lovell 'for her attendance upon us in this time of our sickness'.
Anne's ill health was reflected in gifts to her physician and surgeon.

Anne's will is a remarkable document and demonstrates her kindness
and the fondness which she felt for her household. She made gifts of £10
to each of the gentlemen who attended her, as well as gifts of money to her
yeomen and grooms, and to all the children of her house. Anne remembered
her family and friends, giving to her brother a diamond ring and to her
sister-in-law, the Duchess of Cleves, a ruby ring. Anne bequeathed her
younger sister, Amelia, another diamond ring as well as a further ring to
Catherine, Duchess of Suffolk, who had met her at Deal Castle so many
years before. Anne granted to the Countess of Arundel a ring that she
had, perhaps, acquired from Jane Seymour's jewels when she first arrived
in England which bore the initials 'H' and 'I' (or J). She remembered her
cousin, Count von Waldeck, perhaps to demonstrate that she forgave him
for his complaints about her household, giving him a ruby ring.

Anne left funds for the poor of Bletchingley, Richmond, Hever and Dartford, places in which she had been happiest. Anne's will listed by name nearly everyone in her household and it shows a remarkable memory for details in the former queen. Finally, Anne also remembered her two former stepdaughters, bequeathing to Mary, 'for a remembrance, our best jewel' and, to Elizabeth 'my second best jewel'. Even these gifts were intended to benefit her household and, in recompense for the jewel, Anne asked that Mary would ensure that 'our poor servants may enjoy such small gifts and grants as we have made unto them, in consideration of their long service done unto us'. Elizabeth's jewel was on the condition that the princess took Anne's maid, Dorothy Curzon, into her service. Anne called several members of her household to witness her will in the hope that her wishes would be carried out.

Anne was already nearing her end when she made her will and her last days were spent in her bed at Chelsea, surrounded by the members of the household that she loved. Finally, on 15 July 1557, at the age of only forty-one, the last surviving wife of Henry VIII slipped quietly away with one of her ladies holding her hand. Anne's death caused little stir either in England or on the continent and it was left to her household to mourn her. Although she had long since ceased to be a queen, Anne was still of royal blood and Queen Mary saw it as her duty to provide a suitable funeral for the woman that had once been her stepmother, informing her council that Anne 'shulde be honourably buryed according to the degree of suche an estate'.

Within hours of her death, Anne's body was embalmed and enclosed in a coffin. The coffin was then covered with cloth of gold decorated with Anne's coat of arms and tapers were burned around it both day and night with religious services said daily. According to the London resident and diarist, Henry Machyn:

The iij day of August my lade Anne of Cleyff, sumtyme wyff unto king Henry the viijth cam from Chelsey to be [buried] unto Westmynster, with all the childeryn of Westmynster and [many] prest and clarkes, and then the gray ames [amice] of Powlles and iij crosses, and the monks of Westmynster, and my lord bysshope of Lo[ndon] and my lord abbott of Westmynster rod together next the monks, and then the ij sekturs [executors] ser Edmund Peckham and Ser [Robert] Freston, cofferer to the quen of England; and then my lord admerall, my (lord) Darce of Essex, and many knyghts and gentyllmen; and a-for her servandes, and after her baner of armes; and then her gentyllmen and here hed offesers; and then here charett with viij baners of armes and dyvers armes, and iiij baners of emages of whytt taffeta, wroght with fine gold and her armes; and so by sant James, and so to Chareing-crosse, with a c. Torchys bornyng, her servandes beyrying them, and the xij bed-men of Westmynster had new blake gownes; and they had xij torchys bornyng and iiij whyt branchys and armes; and then ladies and gentyll-women all in blake, and horses; and a viij haroldes of armes in blake, and their horses, and armes sad [set] a-bowt the herse behind and be-for; and iiij harolds baryng the iiij whyt baners; and at (the) churche dore all dyd a-lyght and ther dyd reseyvyd the good lade my lord of London and my lord abbott in ther myteres and copes, sensing her, and ther men dyd bere her with a canapé of blake velvet, with iiij blake stayffes, and so browth in-to the herse and ther tared durge, and so ther all nyght with light bornyng.

The following morning, a requiem mass was performed for Anne and a sermon given. Finally, nearly a month after her death, Anne was carried to her tomb in Westminster Abbey. Once her body was interred, Anne's household officers broke their staves of office as a symbol of the end of their employment and threw them into the tomb. Another mass was held before the mourners departed, leaving Anne of Cleves, fourth wife of Henry VIII in her tomb.

16

How Many Wives Will he Have?

Anne of Cleves was Queen of England for only six months yet it entirely shaped the course of her life and it is as one of the six wives of Henry VIII that she is remembered. She has been described as a nonentity and a woman of little interest historically but the real Anne was so much more than simply the king's 'ugly sister'.

Anne's personal feelings were often at odds with the appearance that she presented to the world and Anne felt that her life was blighted by her marriage to one of the most notorious husbands in history. The shame of the divorce, and her own personal beliefs, caused her to secretly maintain that she was still queen and still married to the king. This was never for love of Henry but simply for the position and security that the role would bring her. Nonetheless, she did become fond of the king during the years of their divorce, as he became fond of her.

Anne is often portrayed as the least significant of Henry's wives. However, she was an international figure of some prominence. After her death, Anne remained a figure of interest, as a letter from the English ambassador to the Emperor Ferdinand during the early years of Elizabeth I's reign records. In the letter the ambassador noted that he was to make enquiries concerning a woman who had appeared in Saxony claiming to be Anne:

> Not long ago I asked how many wives King Henry had really had and how he had treated them. Concerning the Duchess of Cleves [Anne], I have not heard that she was kept a prisoner, but many have told me that she was held

in honour all her life long, and at all times till the day of her death had a free household. I therefore believe that the woman referred to is practising deceit, for I think that were she the sister of the Duke of Cleves, she would have sought refuge with her brother, and not with them of Saxony; nor would she have kept roaming for so long from one place to another in Germany. Your Imperial Majesty durst not therefore put too much confidence in this woman, but I shall immediately write to Your Imperial Majesty whatever I may chance to learn.

The pretender claimed to have been ill-treated in England and sought refuge with Anne's nephew, the Elector of Saxony. Even after death, it was possible for Anne to raise interest internationally, although it quickly became clear to everyone that the pretender was not Anne and she was imprisoned by the Elector, dying in 1560.

Through her marriage and time in England, Anne also opened up an interest in the country among her brother and countrymen. A number of her retinue settled in England, and she built her own court around her. William developed something of a reputation as an Anglophile and, in June 1565, when it was suggested that the Archduke Charles be sent to England to court Elizabeth I, William was identified as the ideal person to accompany him. The Imperial ambassador reported that 'this sight of the Duke of Cleves would gladden and satisfy and predispose the whole country including the commoners, and the queen would willy-nilly be compelled to take the step. A German Prince who speaks only German would not be able to effect much here'. In the end, William was never to visit the country in which his sister settled but he maintained an interest, just as he had done when Anne was alive.

Anne's brother was one of the wealthiest and politically most high-profile German princes and was nicknamed 'William the Rich'. Through his wife, Maria of Austria, he retained the friendship of the Imperial family. He followed his father in favouring a moderate approach to religion and allowed three of his daughters to marry Protestants. In 1566 he suffered a stroke which hampered his ability to rule his duchies but he lived on until 1592, leaving Juliers-Cleves to his only surviving son, John William.

Anne's younger sister, Amelia, also survived her, remaining a spinster at her brother's court until her death in 1586. With William's death, Juliers-Cleves gradually declined and John William died without an heir in 1609, extinguishing the direct line of the house of Mark.

In spite of the difficulties of her position in England, Anne was universally loved. According to the Imperial ambassador who was diligent in his enquiries of Anne's fate: 'I have interrogated a widow who was in the service of the Duchess of Cleves till her death and was endowed by her. She told me that she had held the Duchess's hand when she was expiring. Everybody has nothing but good to say of the Duchess.' Anne won the affection of her household and the people of England through her kindly demeanour.

At the time of Catherine Howard's fall, when Anne was still anticipating a remarriage to the king, one of her ladies exclaimed: 'What a man is this king! How many wives will he have?' It was a question that was on the lips of many in England in the difficult months following Anne's repudiation and, later, Catherine's fall. It was a thought that was on Anne's mind, and she watched Henry VIII's later marital career with increasing anger and desperation. Anne always believed that she was Henry's wife and Henry's widow and his marriage to Catherine Parr was a particular blow. Anne was, perhaps, the luckiest of Henry's wives but the honour of being the luckiest of a pantheon of luckless women did not mean she was happy. Anne remained an exile until the end of her life and Henry VIII blighted her life as he blighted so many others.

Anne of Cleves set out for her marriage with such high hopes and, in the space of less than a year, they were dashed. She remained cheerful and obliging but the rejection was deeply shaming and she never came to terms with her loss. In spite of this, she was loved and Holinshed's Chronicle provides the most suitable epitaph for her: 'a ladie of right commendable regards, courteous, gentle, a good housekeeper, and verie bountifull to hir seruants'. To all the world Henry VIII's widow was Catherine Parr, but to Anne it was always herself. Catherine Parr's death in 1548 left Anne as the last survivor of Henry VIII's six wives, but she will always be remembered simply as his discarded bride.

Notes

L&P refers to *Letters and Papers, Foreign and Domestic of the Reign of Henry VIII*. CSP Spanish refers to *Calendar of State Papers, Spanish*. ACP refers to *Acts of the Privy Council of England*.

1. The Daughter of Cleves

Francesco Coppino to Pope Pius II, 1 June 1461 (Hinds 1912:90) records the marriage of Adolph I to Maria of Burgundy. The Journey of Lev Lord of Rozmital and Blatna in Cust 1909:58 describes Mary of Cleves. The appointment of John I to the Order of the Golden Fleece is in Prospero di Camulio to Francesco Sforza, Duke of Milan, 6 June 1461 (Hinds 1912:95) and in Cust 1909:25. John Paston the Younger to Margaret Paston, 8 July 1468 (Gairdner 1896:318) reports the splendour of the Burgundian court. Adolph I's comments are from Cust 1909:18. The biography of Wilwort of Schaumburg (Cust 1909:175–6) describes Philip of Cleves as hostage. The Visit of Charles V to England, 1522 (Jerdan 1844:60–74) claims that John III was in Charles's train. Midelfort 1994:99 details John II. Charles V's comments on William following his mother's counsel are in Simpson 1862:42. Wotton to Cromwell, 27 April 1540 (L&P15:259) records that William sought counsel from his mother. Wotton's comments on Anne's education are in his letter of 11 August 1539 (Ellis 1824:121–2). Tytler p.258, Strickland 1844:311, Hume p.319 and Weir 2007:385, for example, describe Anne as a Lutheran. Henry VIII's views of Luther are in MacCulloch 1992:167–71. Knecht 1996:164–5 and Duke 1992:148 describe the reformation in Germany. McEntegart 2002:11–2 describes the Diet of Augsburg. The terms of Sibylla's marriage treaty are contained in L&P14 ptII:66–7. Nicholas Wotton and Richard Berde to Cromwell, 3 May 1539 (L&P14 ptI:431) records Olisleger's account of Anne's betrothal to Francis of Lorraine. The marriage treaty is in Bouterwek 1867 (translated by Renate and Stefanie Worden). *Autobiography of Charles V* (Simpson 1862:41–2) contains Charles's comments on Guelders. *The History of the Succession to the Countries of Juliers and Berg* 1738:25 states that Guelders was bequeathed to William. George Nedham (1979:123) mentions troops sent by Henry to Guelders in 1514. Gardiner to Henry VIII, 21 April 1529 (L&P4 ptIII:2415) and Chapuys to Charles V, 25 October 1529 (L&P4 ptIII:2684) record attempts by the German princes to open diplomatic relations with England. Ringk's comments regarding an alliance between England and Cleves are in L&P4 ptIII:2858.

2. A Warren of Honourable Ladies

Cromwell's attempts to find Henry a French bride in 1537 are in Cromwell to Lord William Howard and Gardiner, October 1537 (L&P12 ptII:348). Cromwell to Sir Thomas Wyatt, 30 November 1537 (L&P12 ptII:401) states the offer of the Infanta of Portugal. John Hutton's report of eligible ladies at Brussels is in L&P12 ptII:414. Francis I to Castillon, 11 December 1537 (L&P12 ptII:421-2) and Castillon to Francis I, 30 December 1537 (L&P12 ptII:449) record Henry's desire to marry Mary of Guise. Mary's comments to Peter Mewtas are in Castillon to Francis I, 31 December 1537 (L&P12 ptII:452). Cromwell to Peter Mewtas, February 1538 (Merriman 1902:117-8) contains Henry's instructions regarding Mary. The Duchess of Guise's letter is in L&P13 ptI:54. Henry's conversation with Castillon in May 1538 is in L&P13 ptI:368. Castillon to Montmorency, 31 May 1538 (L&P13 ptI:402) requests new candidates. Castillon to Montmorency, 4 June 1538 (L&P13 ptI:425) and Castillon to Montmorency, 19 June 1538 (L&P13 ptI:450) note the younger Guise sisters. Francis I to Castillon, 10 July 1538 (L&P13 ptI:506) and Castillon to Francis I, 25 July 1538 (L&P13 ptI:535) comment on Henry's request to view the ladies in Calais. Montmorency to Castillon, 29 July 1538 (L&P13 ptI:553) makes the comment about the women not being horses on show. Henry's conversation with Castillon in August 1538 is in L&P13 ptII:28. John Hutton to Cromwell, 9 December 1537 (L&P12 ptII:419) mentions Christina's resemblance to Margaret Shelton. Hutton's description of her appearance is in L&P12 ptII:419. Details of Christina of Denmark's life are in Cartwright 1913 and Iongh 1958. Henry VIII to Wyatt, 22 January 1538 (St Clare Byrne 1968:186) describes the king's decision to honour Christina in marriage. Hutton's Instructions, February 1538 (L&P13 ptII:66) contains Hutton's formal commission. Hutton's conversation with Christina in May 1538 is in L&P13 ptII:375. John Hutton to Cromwell, 26 July 1538 (L&P13 ptII:544) records Christina's interest in England. Wriothesley and Vaughan to Henry, 6 October 1538 (L&P13 ptII:214) reports on Christina's appearance. John Hutton to Henry, 1 April 1538 (L&P13 ptI:251) describes Christina's sober demeanour. Hutton to Cromwell, 14 March 1538 (L&P13 ptI:190) describes the two portraits of Christina. Details of Christina's portrait are in Scharf 1863:106-11. Chapuys to Mary of Hungary, 13 March 1538 (CSP Spanish V ptII:520) recounts Henry's happiness with the portrait. Christina's misgivings are from George Constantine 1831:61. The negotiations for the marriages are in Henry VIII to Wyatt, 5 April 1538 (St Clare Byrne 1968:192-5). Charles's commission to Mary of Hungary to negotiate the marriages is in L&P13

ptI:544. Knecht 1996:204–5 describes the friendship between Charles and Francis. Hutton to Wriothesley, 2 June 1538 (L&P13 ptI:419) describes Hutton's interview with the Regent after the peace with France. Vaughan to Cromwell, 16 December 1538 (L&P13 ptII:457) complains about the Regent's coldness. Wriothesley's Instructions, September 1538 (L&P13 ptII:160–1) records the pressure to be put on Mary of Hungary. Mary's letter to Charles V is in De Iongh 1958:187.

3. The Noblest & Highest Honour

Hall's Chronicle 1904:284 comments on Henry's defensive preparations. McEntegart 2002 discusses relations between England and the League. The German Ambassadors to Henry, 5 August 1538 (L&P13ptII:13) and Franciscus Burgartus Vice-Chancellor and Georgius a Beineburg, Doctor, Oratores, to Cromwell, 5 August 1538 (L&P13 ptII:13) record the debates held in 1538. Henry's letter following the end of the embassy is in L&P13 ptII:194–5. Mont's instructions are in L&P14 ptI:40 and Cromwell to Christopher Mont, January 1539 (Merriman 1902:174–5). Cromwell to Henry, 18 March 1539 (L&P14 ptI:212) contains John Frederick's promise to support the marriage. Henry's instructions to his ambassadors are in L&P14 ptI:191. The ambassadors' complaints that they were unable to get a clear sight of Anne are in Nicholas Wotton and Richard Berde to Cromwell, 3 May 1539 (L&P14 ptI:430). Cromwell to Henry, 24 April 1539 (L&P14 ptI:394) states that John Frederick advised William to arrange the marriage. Nicholas Wotton and Richard Berde to Cromwell, 3 May 1539 (L&P14 ptI:428–31) records the interview with Olisleger on 1 May. Henry's instructions to Dr Peter of July 1539 are in L&P14 ptI:537–8. Holbein's portrait of Anne is discussed in Nichols 1863:72–7 and Chapuys and Mendoza to Charles V, 17 June 1538 (CSP Spanish V ptII:530–1). Nicholas Wotton to Henry VIII, 11 August 1539 (Ellis 1824:122) records that the portraits were good likenesses. *Wriothesley's Chronicle* vol I:85 mentions Cromwell's religious injunctions. John Frederick's letter is in Strype 1822:438–9. Henry's faith is discussed in Bernard 2007:478. The Act of the Six Articles is in Bray 1994:222–3. *Hall's Chronicle* 1904:285 contains the nicknames given to the Act. The Elector of Saxony's letter to the Landgrave of Hesse dated 5 August 1539 is from McEntegart 2002:179. Constantine 1831:60 refers to disappointment in the Act. *Hall's Chronicle* 1904:293–4 details the embassy. William's commission to his ambassadors is in L&P14 ptII:38. Earl of Southampton to Cromwell, 12 September 1539 (L&P14 ptII:45) and Marillac to Francis I, 26 September 1539 (L&P14 ptII:68) mention Henry's enthusiasm. The list of items for the marriage negotiations is in L&P14 ptII:66. The discussion about Anne's dowry is in L&P14 ptII:96–7 and 108. L&P14 ptII:108–9 contains the marriage treaty.

4. Conveyed by Land

The sea voyage is discussed in Ruddock 1961:414–26. Cardinal Farnese's Instructions, 28 November 1539 (L&P14 ptII:211) reports that the pope asked that safe-conduct be denied. The Rutter is printed in Ruddock 1961. Cromwell's Remembrances, September 1539 states that the safe conduct had been requested (L&P14 pyII:110). Henry's letter to Mary of Hungary is in CSP Spanish VI ptI:200–1. Marillac to Francis I, 3 October 1539 (L&P14 ptII:105) records that ships were prepared to escort Anne from Calais. John Husee to Lady Lisle, 27 November 1539 (St Clare Byrne 1981:708, vol V) states that craftsmen were busy in their preparations for Anne. Marillac to Francis I, 25 October 1539 (L&P14 ptII:135) contains Henry's hopes for the marriage. Instructions to prepare Calais are in Cromwell to Lord Lisle, 18 October 1539 (St Clare Byrne 1981:678–9, vol V). The schedule of works there is in L&P15:32–3. Cromwell's Remembrances, October 1539 (L&P14 ptII:150) states 'letters to be written to the Duke, the lady Anne, and the Duchess his mother'. Henry Olisleger to Lord Lisle, 10 November 1539 (St Clare Byrne 1981:703, vol V) records Lady Lisle's gift to Anne. Anthony Denny to Cromwell, 8 October 1539 (L&P14 ptII:112)notes the appointment of Mistress Gilmyn. Nicholas Wotton to Cromwell, 4 December 1539 (L&P14 ptII:231) contains details of 'bruidstuckes'. Marillac to Francis I, 5 November 1539 (L&P14 ptII:170) claims that Henry expected Anne in twenty days. John Husee's comments in October that Anne's arrival was expected are in John Husee to Lord Lisle, 22 October 1539 (St Clare Byrne 1981:685, vol V). Anne Basset's comments are in her letter to Lady Lisle, 5 October 1539 (St Clare Byrne 1981:665, vol V). *Hall's Chronicle* 1904:301 describes Anne's chariot. Anne's train is listed in the *Reception of the Lady Anna of Cleves at Calais, 1539* (Nicholas 1846:172). Wotton to Cromwell, 4 December 1539 (L&P14 ptII:231) describes Anne's journey. Cromwell's Remembrances, November 1539 (L&P14 ptII:176) contain the preparations in Antwerp. The Earl of Southampton and Nicholas Wotton to Henry VIII, 13 December 1539 (L&P14 ptII:247) mention the seditious sermon. Gregory Cromwell to Cromwell, 5 December 1539 (L&P14 ptII:233) reports about the wait in Calais for Anne. The quote from *Holinshed's Chronicle* is in 1808:811. Earl of Southampton and Nicholas Wotton to Henry VIII, 13 December 1539 (L&P14 ptII:247) describes Anne's time at Calais. Southampton's later comments on Anne's appearance are in his deposition (Strype 1822:454). Anne Basset to Lady Lisle, 22 December 1539 (St Clare Byrne 1981:730, vol V) records Lady Lisle's comments on Anne. Cromwell to Southampton, December 1539 (Merriman 1902:243) states that Henry took the delay well. Southampton to Cromwell, 18 December 1539 (L&P14 ptII:259) notes that he opened a packet the letters.

5. A Flanders Mare

Suffolk and Cheyne to Cromwell, 29 December 1539 (L&P14 ptII:283) details the journey to Rochester. Cranmer's letter to Cromwell of 29 December 1539 is in Cox 1846:400. *Hall's Chronicle* 1904:295 contains Anne's reception at Canterbury. *Holinshed's Chronicle* 1808:84 gives Anne's reception at Rochester. Cromwell to Henry VIII, 30 June 1540 (Merriman 1902:268) includes Henry's decision to go to Rochester. *Wriothesley's Chronicle* vol I mentions Henry's disguise. Henry VI was the son of Catherine of Valois, the mother of Edmund Tudor, Henry VIII's grandfather, making Henry VI his great uncle. Henry VI's meeting with Margaret of Anjou is in Report to Bianca Maria Visconti Duchess of Milan, 24 October 1458 (Dockray 2000:15). *Hall's Chronicle* 1904:296 gives one account of the meeting between Henry and Anne. Other accounts used are The Deposition of Sir Anthony Browne (Strype 1822:456–7) and *Wriothesley's Chronicle* vol I. Smollett 1757:635 contains the Flanders Mare comment. Tytler p.264 and Strickland 1844:336 claim that Anne wore a wig and was ugly. Marillac's comments on Anne's appearance are in Marillac to Montmorency, 5 January 1540 (L&P15:10) and Marillac to Francis I, 5 January 1540 (L&P15:10). Lord Russell's comments are in his deposition in Strype 1822:455. Micguel Mercator to Cromwell, 11 November 1539 (L&P14 ptII:178) reported favourably on Anne's appearance. Chapuys to Charles V, 27 July 1543 (CSP Spanish VI ptII:444) and Chapuys to Mary of Hungary, 27 July 1543 (CSP Spanish VI ptII:447) recount Anne's comments on Henry's sixth marriage. Warnicke 2000:145 suggests that Henry's unfavourable reaction might have been due to the possibility that Anne was already married. Lindsey 1995:138 suggests that Henry was unaware that his appearance had declined. Cromwell to Christopher Mont, January 1539 (Merriman 1902:174) states the refusal to provide a portrait of Mary for William. Marillac's Impression of Henry is in Williams 1967:393–4. The *Chronicle of Henry VIII* p.108 describes Anne's comments about Henry's weight. Henry's description of the first meeting is in Burnet 1865:440. The king's New Year's gifts to Anne are described in Anthony Browne's deposition (Strype 1822:457). Henry's conversation with Cromwell is in Cromwell's letter of 30 June 1540 (Merriman 1902:268).

6. A Great Yoke to Enter Into

The main description of the reception is taken from *Hall's Chronicle* 1904:296–301. There are similar descriptions in the Reception of the Lady Anna of Cleves at Calais, 1539 (Nichols 1846:170–1), Marillac to Francis I, 5 January 1540 (L&P15:10), *Holinshed's Chronicle* 1808:811–2, John Norris to Lady Lisle, c.4 January 1540 (St Clare Byrne 1981:7–10) and *Wriothesley's Chronicle* vol I. Cromwell's quote is in his letter to Henry, 12 June 1540 (Merriman 1902:268–9). Cromwell to Henry VIII, 12 June 1540 (Merriman 1902:269) and the Deposition of Thomas Awdleys, Lord Chancellor, Thomas, Archbishop of Canterbury, Thomas, Duke of Norfolk, Charles, Duke of Suffolk, William, Earl of Southampton and Cuthbert Bishop of Durham (Strype 1822) recount the attempts to procure evidence that Anne was free to marry. Warnicke 2000:150–3 states that the ambassadors should have expected to be required to provide evidence of Anne's broken betrothal. Suffolk's comments are in his Deposition

(Strype 1822:453–4). Cromwell to Henry, 12 June 1540 (Merriman 1902:269) comments on the council meeting with the ambassadors. *Autobiography of Charles V* (Simpson 1862:39–40) and Knecht 1996:205–6 describe Charles's visit to France. Herbert 1870:626 records the decision to ask Anne to renounce the betrothal. *Wriothesley's Chronicle* vol II says that Henry and Anne attended Mass together two days before their wedding. Anne's dower is recorded in Jointure of Anne of Cleves (nos.57, 58 and 59) (Hatfield Manuscripts pt I 1883:12). Her household is listed in L&P15:9. Anthony Brown's comments are in his deposition (Strype 1822:457–8).

7. To Satisfy the World

The quote on Anne and Henry's clothes is from *Hall's Chronicle* 1904:302. The Deposition of Sir Anthony Browne (Strype 1822:458) states that Henry took little care in his preparations. Cromwell to Henry VIII, 30 June 1540 (Merriman 1902:270) records the arrangements for Anne to be led into church. *Hall's Chronicle* 1904:302 describes the ceremony. The report of Ladies Rutland, Rochford and Edgecombe is in Strype 1822:462–3. Weir 2007:406 and Fraser 2002:382 comment that Anne was ignorant of sexual relations. Reports on the wedding night are in Henry's declaration (Burnet 1865:430), Cromwell to Henry VIII, 12 June 1540 (Merriman 1902:271) and The Deposition of Sir Thomas Hennege (Strype 1822:458). Henry's concerns over his impotency are in The Deposition of Anthony Denny (Strype 1822:459). The Depositions of Dr Chambers and Dr Butts are in Strype 1822:460–2. The proceedings between Lady Frances Howard and the Earl of Essex are in Abbot 1719. Cromwell to Henry VIII, 30 June 1540 (Merriman 1902:271) records Henry's attempts to consummate the marriage. Anne's attempts to speak to Cromwell are in his letter of 12 June 1540 (Merriman 1902:266). *Hall's Chronicle* 1904:303, records the jousts. Anne's message to her family is in Wotton to Cromwell, 22 February 1540 (L&P15:87). Anne's water pageant is in *Wriothesley's Chronicle* vol I.

8. Queen Anne of Cleves

The King's Works, December 1540 (L&P16:203) record the preparations for Anne at Greenwich. Marillac to Montmorency, 26 March 1540 (L&P15:156) comments on Anne's coronation. Requests for places in Anne's household are in John Gostwyk to Cromwell, 16 November 1539 (L&P15:185) and Jane Rooper to Cromwell, 16 November 1539 (L&P16:185). Olisleger's letter to Lady Lisle, 6 January 1540 is in St Clare Byrne 1981:12, vol VI. For a discussion of Lady Lisle's attempts to secure places for her daughters with Jane Seymour, see Norton 2009. Letters recording Lady Lisle's attempts for Katharine are in Lady Rutland to Lady Lisle, 17 February 1540, Katharine Basset to Lady Lisle, 17 February 1540 and Anne Basset to Lady Lisle, 19 February 1530 (all St Clare Byrne 1981:5–6, 25, 34, vol VI). Marillac's comments on Catherine Howard's appearance are in L&P15:446 and L&P16:5. Richard Hilles to Henry Bullinger, London 1541 (Robinson 1846:201–2, vol I) notes Henry's love for Catherine. The gifts to Anne's train are in L&P15:27. *Hall's Chronicle* 1904:303 states that some of Anne's countrymen stayed. Werner van Hoesteden to Christopher Mont, 16 May 1540 (L&P15:319) records that two of his nephews had entered Henry and Cromwell's service. John Frederick's Letter to Henry is in Strype 1822:437. Vaughan to Cromwell, 15 January 1540 (L&P15:24) comments on Cromwell's letter concerning Henry's relationship with Anne. Wotton to Henry, 22 February 1540 (L&P15:86) records his embassy to Cleves. Wotton to Henry, 9 April 1540 (L&P15:203–5) records William's attempts to negotiate with the emperor. Wotton to Cromwell, 27 April 1540 (L&P15:259) and Wotton to Henry, 30 April 1540 (L&P15:266–7) reports William's meeting with Charles. Henry's instructions to the Scottish ambassador are in L&P15:43. The Queen of Navarre's request for a portrait of Anne is in Wallop to Cromwell, 18 April 1540 (L&P15:244). Sir Richard Ryche to Cromwell, 16 March 1540 (L&P15:138) comments on the foul weather that winter. The creation of Cromwell as Earl of Essex is in L&P15:242–3. The May Day jousts are in L&P15:300 and *Wriothesley's Chronicle* vol I:116–7. John Butler to Henry Bullinger, 24 February 1540 (Robinson 1847:627, vol II) comments on the improved state of religion in England with Anne's arrival.

9. A Special Counsellor of the Match

The quote from Herbert on Cromwell's role in the match is from p.638. Cromwell's life is described in Hutchinson 2007 and Dickens 1959. Chapuys' comments on Cromwell are in Williams 1967:412–3. Cavendish 1962:141 records Cromwell's reaction to the fall of Wolsey. Details of Gardiner's life are in Redworth 1990. Simon Renard to Charles V, 6 November 1553 (CSP Spanish XI:339) contains Gardiner's belief that Cromwell fell because of Anne. Richard Hilles to Henry Bullinger, London 1541 (Robinson 1846:201, vol I) also blames Anne for Cromwell's downfall. Foxe 1965:416–20 discusses Barnes's life. *Hall's Chronicle* 1904:420 describes Gardiner's attack on Barnes on the first Sunday in Lent and Barnes's response. Barnes' recantation is in Burnet 1865:497–8. Scarisbrick 1968:489 describes the disagreement between Cromwell and Norfolk in 1539. The idea that Francis requested Cromwell's fall is suggested by Bernard 2007:565. The pleasure with which reformers greeted Anne's marriage is in John Butler to Henry Bullinger, 24 February 1540 (Robinson 1847:627, vol II). Loades 1994:120 claims that Henry was convinced that Cromwell was responsible for the difficulties in his church. Marillac to Montmorency, 10 April 1540 (L&P15:206) suggests that Cromwell's fall was imminent. The quote claiming that Cromwell's appointment as Earl of Essex was an artifice is from Richard Hilles to Henry Bullinger, London 1541 (Robinson 1846:201–2, vol I). The Deposition of The Earl of Southampton (Strype 1822:454) claims that Cromwell blamed Southampton for the king's reaction to Anne. Cromwell to Wallop, 2 March 1540 (L&P15:119) contains Francis's offer to assist Charles against William if Henry became involved. The Deposition of Thomas Wriothesley

(Strype 1822:459–60) describes his discussions with Cromwell in June regarding the divorce. The arrest of Cromwell is in the *Chronicle of King Henry VIII* p.98–100. Marillac to Montmorency, 23 June 1540 (L&P15:378) gives a similar account. Cranmer's plea for Cromwell is in Cranmer to Henry, 14 June 1540 (Cox 1846:401). The charges against Cromwell are listed in his Bill of Attainder (Williams 1967:487). Herbert 1870:638–40 speaks of the joy felt at Cromwell's arrest and comments that few pitied him. Francis's reaction to Cromwell's fall is in L&P15:373. Marillac to Montmorency, 23 June 1540 (L&P15:377) describes the crowd around Cromwell's house and the inventory of his goods. Cromwell's letter to Henry of 12 June 1540 is in Merriman 1902:264. Cromwell's scaffold speech is in Foxe 1965:402. *Hall's Chronicle* 1904:307 records that Anne was sent to Richmond. Anne's concerns about the move are in Carl Harst to William, 26 June 1540, translated by Renate and Stefanie Worden (Bouterwek 1869:162)

10. Pretended Matrimony

Gardiner's memorandum is in L&P15:387. The notarial statement from Cleves is in L&P15:99. The approach to the Cardinal of Lorraine is in Henry to Wallop, June 1540 (L&P15:397). Kelly 1976:269 describes the divorce. The Earl of Rutland to the Lord Privy Seal, 6 July 1540 (Rutland Manuscripts 1888:27) mentions the events of that morning. All letters from Harst to William have been translated by Renate and Stefanie Worden and are taken from Bouterwek 1869. Harst's indignation is clear from Harst to William of Cleves, 10 July 1540 (p.173). Harst's meeting with the council on 6 July is in Harst to William of Cleves, 7 July 1540 (p.170). Harst to William, 8 July 1540 (p.172) states that Anne was visited by Audeley and Gardiner. Harst to William, Duke of Cleves, 10 July 1540 (p.172) complains of the unjust interrogation of Anne. Henry to Pate, 4 July 1540 (L&P15:413) sets out the official version of events. More and Fisher opposed the king's divorce from Catherine of Aragon (for details see Norton 2008). Henry's commission to investigate the marriage is in L&P15:416. The report of the convocation is in L&P15:429. Herbert 1870:640 names Anne's betrothal to Francis of Lorraine as the cause of the divorce. *Hall's Chronicle* 1904:308 claims that Convocation ruled that both parties were free to marry again. The depositions of the members of Henry's council and household are all from Strype 1822 pp.454–8. Henry's deposition is in Burnet 1865:430. Herbert 1870:640 claims that Henry had secret causes for the divorce that touched Anne's honour. The Commissioners to Henry (Ellis 1824:158–9) states that they informed Anne of the divorce and reported that she was content. Herbert 1870:643 claims that Anne fainted when the commissioners arrived. Harst to William Duke of Cleves, 10 July 1540 (p.173) speaks of Anne's terror and sorrow. Anne's letter to Henry is from Wood 1846:160–2. Henry's reply is from Savage 1949:74–5. Henry to Wallop and Karne, July 1540 (L&P15:440) states that Henry believed Anne was in love with him. Suffolk, Southampton and Wriothesley to Henry, 12 July 1540 (L&P15:437–8) records the negotiations of Anne's divorce settlement. Details of the settlement are in L&P15:446. The settlement is in Hatfield Manuscripts

1883:15. Details of Anne of Cleves' House are in Poole 1996:5 and Godfrey 1924:2–13. Anne's request to see Elizabeth is in Tytler p.279. Henry to Suffolk, Southampton and Wriothesley, 13 July 1540 (L&P15:441) contains the king's insistence that Anne must write to her brother. Anne's letter to her brother is from Hatfield Manuscripts 1883:13–4. Anne of Cleves, July 1540 (L&P15:481) states that Henry intended to keep Anne in England. L&P15:457 contains the return of Anne's wedding ring. Charles's reaction to the divorce is in Richard Pate to Henry, 9 July 1540 (L&P15:434) and Francis's is in Wallop and Carne to Henry, 10 July 1540 (L&P15:436). Sibylla refers to Anne as Queen of England in letters dated 5 August 1547 and 20 September 1553 (Bouterwek and Crecltus 1868:24, 175). McEntegart 2002:202–5 refers to the League's reaction to the divorce. Henry to Clerk and Wotton, 24 July 1540 (L&P15:451) states that Henry had been informed by William that he would be content with justice. William's reaction to the divorce is in Clerk and Wotton to Henry, 11 August 1540 (L&P15:489). Herbert 1870:641 records that William regretted sending Anne to England and was glad she fared no worse. Anne's popularity and the dignified way in which she accepted her divorce is recorded in *Wriothesley's Chronicle* 1875 vol I:119, Marillac to Montmorency, 21 July 1540 (L&P15:447) and Richard Hilles to Henry Bullinger, London 1541 (Robinson 1846:205, vol I). Marillac to Francis I, 6 August 1540 (L&P15:484) records that Henry dined with Anne.

11. That Young Girl Catherine

L&P15:457 records the discharge of Anne's household. Wymond Carew to John Gate, 20 August 1540 (L&P15:494–5) shows the divisions in Anne's household. Privy Council Minutes, 29 August 1540 (Nicholas 1837:18) states that Anne had forwarded a letter from her brother to the council. Richmond Palace is described in Colvin 1982, Cloake 1995, Cloake 2001 and Malden 1911. Cavendish 1962:162 records Henry's exchange of palaces with Wolsey. Chapuys to Mary of Hungary, 8 January 1541 (CSP Spanish VI ptI:305–6) describes Anne's visit to court at New Year. Marillac's comments about Anne's happy reaction to the divorce and her interest in clothes and other pastimes is in Marillac to Montmorency, 15 August 1540 (L&P15:490) and Marillac to Francis I, 3 September 1540 (L&P16:4). Rumours that Henry intended to discard Catherine for Anne are in Marillac to Montmorency, 1 October 1540 (L&P16:57), Pate to the Privy Council, 4 October 1540 (L&P16:61), Marillac to Francis I, 12 January 1540 (L&P16:222) and Chapuys to Mary of Hungary, 17 May 1541 (CSP Spanish VI ptI:328). *Wriothesley's Chronicle* vol I:124 describes Catherine's water pageant. Minutes of the Privy Council on 29 August 1540 and 6 November 1541 refer to plans for Anne's 'sojourning' (Nicholas 1837:18 and 77). Henry's comments on Francis of Lorraine's marriage are from Chapuys to Mary of Hungary, 18 June 1541 (CSP Spanish VI ptI:333). The Council to William Paget, 12 November 1541 (Herbert 1870:652) describes Catherine's arrest. Catherine's confession is in Bath Manuscripts 1907:9. The *Chronicle of Henry VIII* p.82 records that Culpeper and Catherine were in love before her marriage. Her letter to Culpeper is in Crawford

2002:210. Confession of Margyt Morton (L&P16:618) records Catherine's orders that her ladies were not to enter her bedchamber. The rumours that Anne had borne the king a son are in Chapuys to Charles V, 11 December 1541 (CSP Spanish VI ptI:413-4). The investigation into this is in Strickland 1844:358 and Council with the King, 9 December 1541 (L&P16:670). The Privy Council's judgment on the matter is in Nicholas 1837:279. Jane Rattsay's comments are in L&P16:655. Chapuys to Charles V, 19 November 1541 (CSP Spanish VI ptI:396) states that Anne rejoiced at Catherine's fall. Olisleger's letters to Southampton and Cranmer are in L&P16:634 and 635. Southampton and Cranmer's reactions are in L&P16:674 and 676 respectively. The approach to Marillac for assistance in Anne's reinstatement and the Queen of Navarre's comments are in Marillac to the Queen of Navarre, 17 January 1542 (L&P17:17). Marillac to Francis I, 17 March 1542 (L&P17:80-1) comments that the Catherine Howard debacle aged Henry. Catherine's Bill of Attainder is in Williams 1967:488. Chapuys to Charles V, 25 February 1542 (CSP Spanish vol VI ptI:471) records Catherine's time in the Tower and her death. *Chronicle of Henry VIII* p.86 claims Catherine said on the scaffold that she wished to die Culpeper's wife.

12. The King's Sister

The Remonstrance of Anne of Cleves is in Macray 1883. Paget to Henry, 26 January 1542 (L&P17:21) sent a copy of the book to Henry. Paget to Henry, 26 February 1542 (L&P17:53) contains Paget's conversation with Francis over the book. Chapuys to Charles V, 25 March 1542 (L&P17:89) recounts that Henry sent his doctors to tend to Anne in her sickness. Knecht 1996:207 discusses William's French alliance. The quote is from Chapuys to Granvelle, 10 August 1542 (CSP Spanish vol VI ptII:90). Marillac to Francis I, 1 August 1542 (L&P17:323) records the concern of the English merchants over the safety of Antwerp. Knecht 1996:213 records Henry's pact with Charles. Wallop to the Council, 10 October 1542 (L&P17:530) discusses William's losses. William's financial difficulties are in Paget to Henry VIII, 14 December 1542 (in L&P17:663). Charles V's Manifesto against the Duke of Cleves is in CSP Spanish Vol VI ptII:304-5. Chapuys to Charles V, 9 February 1542 (CSP Spanish vol VI ptI:468) contains the quote showing Henry's interest in ladies of his court. Chapuys to Charles V, 16 March 1543 (CSP Spanish vol VI ptI:278) and Chapuys to Mary of Hungary, 17 March 1543 (L&P18 ptI:162) recount Anne's visit to court in March 1543. Anne's treatment in January 1543 is in Chapuys to Charles V, 15 January 1543 (L&P18 ptI:30). Mary's expenses record her visit to Richmond (Madden 1831:118-9). Henry's sixth marriage is described in a notarial statement in L&P18 ptI:483. The Lords of the Council to Wymond Carew, 27 July 1543 in L&P Addenda vol I pt II:541-2 records Henry's visit to Richmond. Anne's reaction to the marriage is from Chapuys to Charles V, 27 July 1542 (CSP Spanish vol VI ptII:444) and Chapuys to the Queen of Hungary, 27 July 1543 (CSP Spanish vol VI ptII:447). William's defeat at Heneberge is in Seymour and Wotton to Henry, 24 June 1543 (L&P18 ptI:431). Wotton to Henry, 21 July 1543 (L&P18 ptI:502) reports that

Charles's return to the Low Countries. Attempts to get William's ambassador expelled from England are in Chapuys to Charles V, 27 July 1543 (L&P18 ptI:513). Christopher Mont to Henry, 9 August 1543 (L&P18 ptII:13) contains Charles's response to attempts to intercede for William at Spire. Wallop and Others to Henry, 13 August 1543 (L&P18 ptII:21) states that Charles had entered Juliers and recounts the fall of Duren. The Prince of Orange's success in Juliers is in Wotton to Henry, 30 August 1543 (L&P18 ptII:48). The death of Anne's mother is in Bonner to Henry, 3 September 1543 (L&P18 ptII:68) and Wotton to Henry, 6 September 1543 (L&P18 ptII:76). William's submission is in Treaty of Peace between Charles V and the Duke of Cleves, 7 September 1543 (CSP Spanish vol VI ptII:476). Mary of Hungary, 10 September 1543 (L&P18 ptII:86) states that William's army joined Charles's to attack France. Treaty of Crespi, 18 September 1544 (L&P20 ptI:129) sets out the peace between Francis and Charles. Anne's wedding gift to William is in L&P21 ptI:566. Albert, Duke of Prussia, to Henry, 16 October 1543 (L&P18 ptII:161) and Henry to Albert, Duke of Prussia, 8 January 1544 (L&P19 ptI:7) record the gift of the white osprey. Anne's visit to court in March 1546 is in Scepperus to Schore, 28 March 1546 (L&P21 ptI:225). Reports that Anne came and went to court as she pleased are in John Dymocke to Vaughan, 26 May 1546 (L&P21 ptI:457). The King's Court, May 1564 (L&P21 pt:479) lists Anne as one of the members of the court. John Dymock, 23 May 1546 (L&P21 ptI:436) claims that Anne had borne Henry two children. Grants in May 1546 (L&P21 ptI:485) list the surveys of Anne's goods. Anne's presence at the reception for the French Admiral is in L&P21 vol I:693–6.

13. Everything is so Costly Here

John Fowler's conversation with Edward VI is in Nichols 1862:cxv–cxvi.. Tudor inflation is considered in Outhwaite 1969. A Discussion on the Coinage, 1553, by Sir John Price (Williams 1967:1019) notes the debasement of the coinage. Henry's generosity to Anne is recorded in a number of payment records, including L&P20 ptII:184 and 516 and L&P21 ptII:407. The Queen Dowager to Van Der Delft, 1 April 1547 (CSP Spanish IX:65) records Mary of Hungary's request for news of Anne. William's letter of Credence to his ambassador are in Turnbull 1861a:7, 81 and 117. Anne's petition to the Privy Council in April 1547 is in ACPII:80–3. Henry's grant of the reversion of Bletchingley to Cawarden is in L&P21 ptII:341–2. Cawarden is described in Kempe 1836:15. The letter regarding Bletchingley is in ACPII:471–2. Cawarden paid rent to Anne as is recorded in an Acquitance from the Lady Anne of Cleves to Sir Thomas Cawarden, Knight, for Rents of Bletchingley and her Lands There, 30 December 1553 (Kempe 1836:10). His changes to Bletchingley church are in Churchwardens' Account for the Parish Church of Bletchingley, 1552 (Kempe 1836:162–4). Anne's visit to Cawarden's London house is the expenses listed in Kempe 1836:10–4. Anne's visit to court in May 1548 to discuss Richmond is in Van Der Delft to Charles V, 16 May 1548 (CSP Spanish IX:266). The works carried out by the king at Bletchingley are in Colvin 1982:229. Privy Council, 3 April 1552 (ACPIV:12) records the surrender of Bisham. Anne's letter to Princess Mary is in Crawford 2002:204–5. Attempts to force Anne to exchange her lands in Kent are in Privy Council, 21 May 1552 (ACPV:52). Somerset's time as Protector and Edward VI's reign are described in Jordan 1970. The *Diary of Henry Machyn* (Nichols 1848) comments on Somerset's fall. Anne's letter is quoted from Jordan 1970:104. Anne's desire to return to Cleves is noted in CSP Spanish X:282. CSP Spanish X:323 reports that Dr Cruser received a favourable response from the council. Anne's petition to the council in August 1552 is in ACPV:109. Privy Council, 8 April 1553 (ACPV:250) records payments made to Anne. The reference to Anne being in debt is in Privy Council, 29 June 1550 (ACPIII:60). Anne's petition for John Frederick's release is in Charles V to Van Der Delft, 15 November 1547 (CSP Spanish IX:203–4). Privy Council, 23 July 1552 (ACPIV:100) notes John Frederick's release.

14. Favourable Treatment

The struggle for the crown between Jane and Mary is in *Chronicle of Queen Jane and Two Years of Queen Mary* (Nichols 1849:1–13). Mary's coronation is described in Knighton 1998:9–11, *Chronicle of Queen Jane* (Nichols 1849:27–30), *Wriothesley's Chronicle* vol II:103, *Vita Mariae Angliae Reginae* (MacCulloch 1984:275–6). The pageants at Mary's coronation are described in *The Chronicle of Queen Jane* (Nichols 1849:29). Mary's coronation banquet is in *Diary of Henry Machyn* (Nichols 1848:45–6). The Ambassadors in England to Charles V, 27 August 1553 (CSP Spanish XI:188) describe the early changes to religion under Mary. Mary's attempts to return England to the Catholic faith are detailed in Loades 1989:193–4. Anne's support for the Archduke Ferdinand is in Simon Renard to Charles V, 15 October 1553 (CSP SpanishXI:300). Simon Renard to Charles V, 14 November 1553 (CSP SpanishXI:357–8) states that the King of the Romans sent an ambassador to speak for his son. Charles' attempts to disrupt Ferdinand's suit are in Prescott 2003:266. Renard's conversation with Gardiner following Mary's engagement is in his dispatch of 6 November 1553 (CSP SpanishXI:338). Wyatt's rebellion is described in *The History of Wyatt's Rebellion* (Pollard 1903:208) and *Chronicle of Queen Jane* (Nichols 1849:39–40). Wyatt's proclamation is in Pollard 1903:212–3. Mary's speech is on p.240 of the same source. Simon Renard to Charles V, 12 February 1554 (CSP SpanishXII:94) records Mary's suspicions about Anne's involvement. Simon Renard to Charles V, 8 February 1554 (CSP SpanishXII:89), Lord Paget to Simon Renard, 23 December 1553 and Lord Paget to Simon Renard, 29 December 1553 (both Beer and Jack 1974:105) recount French hostility to Mary's marriage. Charles V to Simon Renard, 18 February 1554 (CSP SpanishXII:117) contains fears that William and Elizabeth were allied with France. Cawarden's account of his movements during the rebellion is in Cawarden's Petition to Elizabeth's Council (Kempe 1836:140). Letters under the Queen's signet and sign manual, commanding Sir Thomas Cawarden to prepare himself, his servants, and his tenants, to march at an hour's notice against the rebels are in Kempe 1836:132. The decision to seize Cawarden's armoury is in Lord William Howard to the

Sheriff, 29 January 1554 (Kempe 1836:133). Cawarden's armoury is itemised in Kempe 1836:135–9. Elizabeth's letter to Cawarden is in Kempe 1836:171. Simon Renard to Charles V, 3 April 1554 (CSP SpanishXII:203) reports that Dr Cruser brought William's congratulations. The marriage of Mary and Philip is described in a letter of John Elder's (Nichols 1849:137–43) and in the official account recorded by the English heralds (Nichols 1849:167–9). Anne's letter to Queen Mary is in Crawford 2002:205.

15. Departed This Life at Chelsea

Anne's attempts to annul her divorce are in CSP Spanish XI:279. Simon Renard to Charles V, 3 April 1554 (CSP SpanishXII:203–4) and William of Cleves to Mary I, 14 March 1554 (Turnbull 1861:66) report the deaths of John Frederick and Sibylla. Dr Wotton to Petre, 1555 (Turnbull 1861:200) details Diaceto's dismissal. Diaceto's claim for sums due is in Knighton 1998:74–5. Fraser 2002:501 and Warnicke 2000:253–4 detail the dispute within Anne's household. William to Mary I, 5 August 1556 (Turnbull 1861:245) asks the queen to dismiss Anne's three servants. The Council to the king, 10 September 1556 (Knighton 1998:237) reports on the investigations into Anne's servants. Philip's response is in Knighton 1998:238. The Privy Council's reports of the dismissal of Anne's servants are in ACPV:353, 354 and 362. Sir Thomas Cornwaleys to Sir William Cecil, 29 April 1557 (Salisbury Manuscripts 1883:140–1) complains of Anne's stubbornness in a property exchange. Anne's will is in Strickland 1844:364–7. *Holinshed's Chronicles* vol IV:88 and *Wriothesley's Chronicle* vol II:138 contain Anne's death. Mary's order that Anne be given a royal funeral is in ACPVI:128. The preparations for Anne's funeral are in *Excerpta Historica* p.313. The *Diary of Henry Machyn* (Nichols 1848:145–6) describes Anne's funeral.

16. How Many Wives Will he Have?

Loades 2009:112 describes Anne as a nonentity, for example. Anne is little written about with the only other biography of her being Saaler 1997. The quote from the Imperial ambassador is in Baron Breuner to the Emperor Ferdinand, 8 September 1559 (Klarwill 1928:121–2). Suggestions that William be sent to England with the Archduke Charles are in Report of Zwetkovich to the Emperor Maximilian, 4 June 1565 (Klarwill 1928:231). Details of William's life are from Midelfort 1994:94. The extinction of the House of Mark is noted in Knecht 1996:569. The quote from one of Anne's ladies is in L&P16:655. *Holinshed's Chronicles* vol IV:88 praise Anne.

Bibliography

Primary Sources

Acts of the Privy Council of England, New Series, vols I–VI, ed. Dasent, J.R., (London, 1890–1893)

Bath Manuscripts: *Historical Manuscripts Commission: Calendar of the Manuscripts of the Marquis of Bath,* vol II (Dublin, 1907)

Beer, B.L. and Jack, S.M. (ed.) *The Letters of William, Lord Paget, 1547–63* (Camden Miscellany XXV, 1974)

Bentley, S., (ed.), *Excerpta Historica* (London, 1833)

Bouterwek, A.W. and Creclius, W. (eds.), 'Briefe der Herzogin Sibylla Von Julich-Cleve-Berg an Ihren Gemahl Johann Friedrich den Grossmuthigen, Churfursten Von Sachsen' in *Zeitschrift des Bergischen Geschichtsvereins* 5 (1868)

Bouterwek, A.W., 'Anna Von Cleve' in *Zeitschrift Des Bergischen Geschihtsverin* 4 (1867)

Bouterwek, A.W., 'Anna Von Cleve' in *Zeitschrift Des Bergischen Geschichtsvereins* 6 (1869)

Bray, G. (ed.), *Documents of the English Reformation* (Cambridge, 1994)

Burnet, G., (ed.), *The History of the Reformation of the Church of England,* vol IV (Oxford, 1865)

Calendar of State Papers Domestic Series of the Reign of Mary I, ed. Knighton, C.S. (London, 1998)

Calendar of State Papers and Manuscripts Existing in the Archives and Collections of Milan, vol I, ed. Hinds, A.B. (London, 1912)

Calendar of State Papers, Foreign Series, of the Reign of Edward VI, ed. Turnbull, W.B. (London, 1861)

Calendar of State Papers, Foreign Series, of the Reign of Mary I, ed. Turnbull, W.B. (London, 1861)

Calendar of State Papers, Spanish vols V-XII, eds., De Gayangos, P., Hume, M.A.S., and Tyler, R. (London,1888–1949)

Cavendish, G., *Thomas Wolsey Late Cardinal His Life and Death* (London, 1962)

Constantine, G., *Transcript of an Original Manuscript, Containing a Memorial from George Constantyne to Thomas Lord Cromwell*, ed. Amyot, T. (Archaeologia 23, 1831)

Cranmer, T., *Miscellaneous Writings and Letters*, ed. Cox, J.E. (Cambridge, 1846)

Crawford, A. (ed.), *Letters of the Queens of England* (Stroud, 2002)

Dockray, K. (ed.), *Henry VI, Margaret of Anjou and the Wars of the Roses: A Source Book* (Stroud, 2000)

Ellis, H. (ed.), *Original Letters Illustrative of English History*, vol II (London, 1824)

Foxe, J., *The Acts and Monuments of John Foxe*, vol V (New York, 1965)

Gairdner, J. (ed.), *The Paston Letters*, vol II (Westminster, 1896)

Hall, E., *The Triumphant Reigne of Kyng Henry the VIII*, vol II (London, 1904)

Hinds, A.B., *Calendar of State Papers and Manuscripts Existing in the Archives and Collections of Milan, vol I 1385–1618* (London, 1912)

Holinshed's Chronicles of England, Scotland and Ireland, vols III and IV (London, 1808)

Hume, M.A.S. (ed.), *Chronicle of King Henry VIII of England* (London, 1889)

Jerdan, W., (ed.), *Original Documents Illustrative of the Courts and Times of Henry VII and Henry VIII Selected from the Private Archive of his Grace the Duke of Rutland* (London, 1842)

Kempe, A.J. (ed.), *The Loseley Manuscripts and Other Rare Documents* (London, 1836)

Klarwill, V., von, (ed.), *Queen Elizabeth and Some Foreigners* (London, 1928)

Letters and Papers, Foreign and Domestic, of the Reign of Henry VIII, vols IV–XXI and Addenda vol I pt II, eds., Brewer, J.S., Gairdner, J., Brodie, R.H. (London, 1876–1932)

Madden, F., (ed.), *Privy Purse Expenses of the Princess Mary* (London, 1831)

Merriman, R.B., (ed.), *Life and Letters of Thomas Cromwell*, 2 vols (Oxford, 1902)

Nedham, G., *The Politics of a Tudor Merchant Adventurer: A Letter to the Earls of East Friesland*, ed. Ramsay, G.D. (Manchester, 1979)

Nicolas, H, (ed.), *Proceedings and Ordinances of the Privy Council of England*, vol VII (London, 1837)

Nichols, J.G., (ed.), *The Chronicle of Calais* (London, 1846)

___, (ed.), *The Diary of Henry Machyn* (London, 1848)

___, (ed.), *The Chronicle of Queen Jane and of Two Years of Queen Mary* (London, 1849)

___, (ed.), *Literary Remains of King Edward the Sixth* (London, 1862)

Pollard, A.F., (ed.), *Tudor Tracts* (Westminster, 1903)

Robinson, H., (ed.), *Original Letters Relative to the English Reformation*, 2 vols (Cambridge, 1847)

Rutland Manuscripts: *Historical Manuscripts Commission, Twelfth Report, Appendix, Part IV: The Manuscripts of his Grace the Duke of Rutland, vol I* (London, 1888)

Salisbury Manuscripts: *Historical Manuscripts Commission: Calendar of the Manuscripts of the Marquis of Salisbury Preserved at Hatfield House, Hertfordshire,* part I (London, 1883)

Savage, H., (ed.), *The Love Letters of Henry VIII* (London, 1949)

Simpson, L.F. (ed.), *The Autobiography of Charles V* (London, 1862)

St Clare Byrne, M. (ed.), *The Letters of King Henry VIII* (London, 1968)

___, (ed.), *The Lisle Letters,* vols V and VI (Chicago, 1981)

Strype, J., (ed.), *Ecclesiastical Memorials,* vol I pt II (1822)

Williams, C.H. (ed.), *English Historical Documents, vol V* (London, 1967)

Wingfield, R., *The Vita Mariae Angliae Reginae,* ed. MacCulloch, D. (Camden Miscellany XXVIII, 1984)

Wood, M.A.E. (ed.), *Letters of Royal and Illustrious Ladies,* vol II (London, 1846)

Wriothesley, C., *A Chronicle of England During the Reigns of the Tudors,* 2 vols ed. Hamilton, W.D. (London, 1875)

Secondary Sources

Bernard, G.W., *The King's Reformation* (London, 2007)

Cartwright, J., *Christina of Denmark Duchess of Milan and Lorraine* (London, 1913)

Cloake, J., *Palace and Parks of Richmond and Kew,* vol I (London, 1995)

___, *Richmond Palace Its History and Its Plan* (Richmond, 2001)

Colvin, H.M., *The History of the King's Works,* vol IV (London, 1982)

Cust, H., *Gentlemen Errant: Being the Journeys and Adventures of Four Noblemen in Europe During the Fifteenth and Sixteenth Century* (London, 1909)

Dickens, A.G., *Thomas Cromwell and the English Reformation* (London, 1959)

Duke, A., 'The Netherlands', in Pettegree, A., (ed.), *The Early Reformation in Europe* (Cambridge, 1992)

Fraser, A., *The Six Wives of Henry VIII* (London, 2002)

Godfrey, W.H., *Anne of Cleves' House, Southover, Lewes* (1924)

Guy, J., *Tudor England* (Oxford, 1988)

Herbert, E., *The History of England under Henry VIII* (London, 1870)

Hume, M., *The Wives of Henry the Eighth* (London)

Hutchinson, R., *Thomas Cromwell* (London, 2007)

Iongh, J., de, *Mary of Hungary* (London, 1958)

Jordan, W.K., *Edward VI: The Threshold of Power* (London, 1970)

Kelly, H.A., *The Matrimonial Trials of Henry VIII* (Stanford, 1976)

Knecht, R.J., *The Rise and Fall of Renaissance France* (London, 1996)

Lindsey, K., *Divorced Beheaded Survived* (1995)

Loades, D., *Mary Tudor* (Oxford, 1989)

___, *Henry VIII and his Queens* (Stroud, 1994)

___, *The Tudor Queens of England* (London, 2009)

Malden, H.E. (ed.), *The Victoria History of the Counties of England: Surrey, vol III* (London, 1911)

MacCulloch, D., 'England', in Pettegree, A., (ed.), *The Early Reformation in Europe* (Cambridge, 1992)

Mackray, W.D., *The "Remonstrance" of Anne of Cleves* (Archaeologia 47, 1883)

McEntegart, R., *Henry VIII, The League of Schmalkalden and the English Reformation* (Woodbridge, 2002)

Midelfort, H.C.E., *Mad Princes of Renaissance Germany* (Charlottesville, 1994)

Nichols, J.G., *Remarks upon Holbein's Portraits of the Royal Family of England, and more Particularly upon the Several Portraits of the Queens of Henry the Eighth* (Archaeologia 39, 1863)

Norton, E., *Anne Boleyn, Henry VIII's Obsession* (Chalford, 2008)

___, *Jane Seymour, Henry VIII's True Love* (Chalford, 2009)

Outhwaite, R.B., *Inflation in Tudor and Early Stuart England* (London, 1969)

Poole, H., *Anne of Cleves House and Museum* (1996)

Prescott, H.F.M., *Mary Tudor: The Spanish Tudor* (London, 2003)

Redworth, G., *In Defence of the Church Catholic: The Life of Stephen Gardiner* (Oxford, 1990)

Ruddock, A., *The Earliest Original English Seaman's Rutter and Pilot's Chart* (The Journal of the Institute of Navigation 14, 1961)

Saaler, M., *Anne of Cleves* (London 1997)

Scarisbrick, J.J., *Henry VIII* (Harmondsworth, 1968)

Scharf, G., *Remarks on a Portrait of the Duchess of Milan, Recently Discovered at Windsor Castle, Probably Painted by Holbein at Brussels in the Year 1538* (Archaeologia 39, 1863)

Smollett, T., *A Complete History of England,* vol II (London, 1757)

Strickland, A., *Lives of the Queens of England,* vol IV (London, 1844)

The History of the Succession of the Countries of Juliers and Berg (London, 1738)

Tytler, S., *Tudor Queens and Princesses* (1896)

Warnicke, R.M., *The Marrying of Anne of Cleves* (Cambridge, 2000)

Weir, A., *The Six Wives of Henry VIII* (London, 2007)

List of Illustrations

26. Thomas Cromwell. © Jonathan Reeve JR960b53p283 15001600.
27. Thomas Howard, Duke of Norfolk. © Jonathan Reeve JR949b2p110 15001550.
28 and 29. Two views of Richmond Palace, first by Hollar *c.*1650 and in a later engraving. © Jonathan Reeve JR1112b67plviii 16001650 and © Elizabeth Norton.
30 and 31. Richmond Palace today. © Elizabeth Norton.
32. A Pageant Design for Anne Boleyn's Coronation by Holbein. © Elizabeth Norton.
33. Anne Boleyn by Holbein. © Elizabeth Norton.
34. Little now remains of Anne's second residence Bletchingley Palace. © Elizabeth Norton.
35. Catherine of Aragon. © Jonathan Reeve JR820b53p87 15001600.
36. Anne of Cleves' House, Lewes. © Elizabeth Norton.
37. The fine gardens at Anne of Cleves' House, Lewes. © Elizabeth Norton.
38. The Priest's House, West Hoathly, Sussex. © Elizabeth Norton.
39. Hever Castle, Kent. © David Sawtell.
40. Anne's signature. © Elizabeth Norton.
41. Catherine Howard. © Elizabeth Norton.
42. Princess Mary. © Jonathan Reeve JR997b66fp40A 15001600.
43. Catherine Howard as the Queen of Sheba. © Elizabeth Norton.
44. Catherine Parr in a window at the chapel at Sudeley Castle. © Elizabeth Norton.
45. Edward VI. © Elizabeth Norton.
46. Edward Seymour, Duke of Somerset. © Elizabeth Norton.
47. The tomb of Thomas Cawarden in Bletchingley Church. © Elizabeth Norton.
48. Bletchingley Church. © Elizabeth Norton.
49. Mary I. © Jonathan Reeve JR1019b66fp8 15001600.
50. Philip II of Spain. © Jonathan Reeve JR1051b66fp72 15001600.
51 and 52. Elizabeth I. © Jonathan Reeve JR1114b66pviii 15501600 and © Jonathan Reeve JR1116b66fp16B 15001550.
53 and 54. Westminster Abbey. © Elizabeth Norton and © Jonathan Reeve JR1116b66fp16B 15001550.

Index

Index

Tudor History from Amberley Publishing

THE TUDORS
Richard Rex

'The best introduction to England's most important dynasty'
DAVID STARKEY
'Gripping and told with enviable narrative skill... a delight'
THES
'Vivid, entertaining and carrying its learning lightly'
EAMON DUFFY
'A lively overview' **THE GUARDIAN**

£20.00 978-1-84868-049-4 272 pages HB 143 illus., 64 col

CATHERINE HOWARD
Lacey Baldwin Smith

'A brilliant, compelling account' **ALISON WEIR**
'A faultless book' **THE SPECTATOR**
'Lacey Baldwin Smith has so excellently caught the
atmosphere of the Tudor age' **THE OBSERVER**

£9.99 978-1-84868-521-5 256 pages PB 25 col illus

MARGARET OF YORK
Christine Weightman

'A pioneering biography of the Tudor dynasty's most
dangerous enemy'
PROFESSOR MICHAEL HICKS
'Christine Weightman brings Margaret alive once more'
THE YORKSHIRE POST
'A fascinating account of a remarkable woman'
THE BIRMINGHAM POST

£14.99 978-1-84868-099-9 208 pages PB 40 illus

THE SIX WIVES OF HENRY VIII
David Loades

'Neither Starkey nor Weir has the assurance and command
of Loades' **SIMON HEFFER, LITERARY REVIEW**
'Incisive and profound. I warmly recommend this book'
ALISON WEIR

£9.99 978-1-4456-0049-9 256 pages PB 55 illus, 31 col

ANNE BOLEYN	MARY BOLEYN	JANE SEYMOUR	HENRY VIII	ELIZABETH I
Elizabeth Norton	Josephine Wilkinson	Elizabeth Norton	Richard Rex	Richard Rex
£9.99 978-1-84868-514-7	£9.99 978-1-84868-525-3	£9.99 978-1-84868-527-7	£9.99 978-1-84868-098-2	£9.99 978-1-84868-423-2
224 pages PB 55 illus, 36 col	208 pages PB 22 illus, 10 col	224 pages PB 53 illus, 26 col	192 pages PB 81 illus, 48 col	192 pages PB 75 illus

THE EARLY LOVES OF ANNE BOLEYN	CATHERINE PARR	ANNE OF CLEVES	ANNE BOLEYN
Josephine Wilkinson	Elizabeth Norton	Elizabeth Norton	P. Friedmann
£20.00 978-1-84868-430-0	£18.99 978-1-84868-582-6	£20.00 978-1-84868-329-7	£20.00 978-1-84868-827-8
224 pages HB 34 illus, 17 col	320 pages HB 52 illus, 39 col	224 pages HB 54 illus, 27 col	352 pages HB 47 illus, 20 col

Available from all good bookshops or to order direct
Please call **01285-760-030 www.amberleybooks.com**